A
SEASON *for*
JUSTICE

A
SEASON *for*
JUSTICE

DEFENDING THE RIGHTS OF THE
CHRISTIAN HOME, CHURCH, AND SCHOOL

DAVID FRENCH

COUNSEL FOR INTERVARSITY
CHRISTIAN FELLOWSHIP'S RELIGIOUS
FREEDOM CRISIS TEAM

BROADMAN
& HOLMAN
PUBLISHERS

NASHVILLE, TENNESSEE

0-8054-2491-1

Published by Broadman & Holman Publishers,
Nashville, Tennessee

Subject Heading: CHURCH \ CHRISTIAN LIFE

1 2 3 4 5 6 7 8 9 10 06 05 04 03 02

DEDICATION

*To Pastor Stanley Holder and the members of
Trinity Assembly of God*

*To Curtis and Jody Chang and the Senior Leaders of the
Tufts Christian Fellowship*

Thank you for your wisdom and courage.

TABLE OF CONTENTS

INTRODUCTION

"I'm telling you, David, everything has changed."

It was three weeks after September 11, 2001, and I was driving from a rural airport with a client from North Carolina. As the miles rolled by, we passed several public high schools and elementary schools, and each one of them bore a sign that read "God Bless America." At city halls and firehouses, flags flew high and hand-painted signs asked for God to bless our nation, the victims of September 11, and the soldiers who would soon fight to protect us all. My friend and client related how his church, once half-empty, now had to pull folding chairs from storage to accommodate all the new worshipers. He told me how coworkers who had once ridiculed his faith now turned to him for comfort. To my friend—and to thousands if not millions of other Christians—the message was clear: America was returning to the God of its fathers.

Christian after Christian had the same thought: "Things have changed." After long, losing battles against the great tides of secular humanism, multicultural liberal orthodoxy, and sexual politics, the tide had turned. "Now," people said, "they can't ignore God. Now they can't tell us we don't need prayer in schools, that Christians are bigoted and hateful, and that all worldviews are equally valid. Now they need the eternal comfort, the perfect peace, and the moral courage that Christ has to offer. Our voices, mocked for so many years, will finally be heard."

1

And for a few days, even for a few weeks, those Christians were correct. In the days that followed September 11, I watched national news reporters weep as they covered prayer services and funerals. I watched as commentators and pundits who had previously shunned conservative Christians eagerly welcomed Christian guests to their radio and televisions shows and nodded along gravely as these same Christians described the need for the nation to look to God for support. National magazines and newspapers asked if Americans would any longer be interested in the same kinds of entertainment, the same kinds of relationships. Many of us watched, amazed, as the nation raised up a new kind of hero—one famous not for beauty or screen charisma but for courage and self-sacrifice. For once, the Todd Beamers of the world received more press attention, more adulation than Tom Cruise, Madonna, or Britney Spears.

More than one Christian even asked me if September 11 meant an end to the culture wars—an end to the religious conflict that had driven so many Christians to the margins of American society. With a nation so keenly aware of its need for God and God's blessing, was the battle for religious freedom even relevant? Wouldn't Americans be more concerned with attending a church than closing it? Wouldn't Americans be more concerned with listening to the gospel than silencing it? Wouldn't they see that multicultural-identity politics and sexual liberation are cold comforts when confronted with the reality of sorrow, death, and eternity?

And yet . . . as I responded to those questions, I thought about my own experiences. I thought about the college protestors who scrawled anti-Christian grafitti on campus buildings and silently stared down Christians when those Christians had the audacity to fight for their right to exist on campus. I thought about the local government official who once snarled at me, "We can and will define how you worship God." I thought about the profanities and threats unleashed against me when I once tried to write a letter objecting to my law school's policy of paying for elective abortions. I remembered the pain and hurt as Christian high school and college students described the rejection and mockery they experienced on a near-daily basis. And I remembered countless impassioned arguments with gay rights advocates, radical feminists, and leading liberal scholars—arguments that began in classrooms and spilled over into hallways, restaurants, offices, and courts across the country.

As my thoughts turned to these experiences, and as I read closely the writings of leading liberal politicians and intellectuals, I realized that the battle is far from over. September 11 did not represent a termination of cultural hostilities. At best, it caused a truce—a temporary cease-fire—as Americans united to fight a common enemy. Evangelical Christians and cultural liberals still have incompatible worldviews. Evangelical Christians and cultural liberals still believe that their view is correct, and both sides want to turn an entire nation into a reflection of their own worldview.

While the conflict still exists, the language has changed. Christians who once were denounced as dangerous zealots because of their opposition to abortion or the latest gay rights initiative are now regarded as dangerous because they represent just one strain of "fundamentalism" that threatens to plunge the "enlightened" secular world into chaos. To truly defeat the threat of world terrorism and Islamic extremism, cultural liberals argue that we must embrace secularism, not Christianity. We must further separate church from state. Islam may not be the enemy, but religion—particularly "fundamental" or "conservative" religion—most certainly is. America is great not because of its Christianity or its religiosity but because it has either cleansed itself of that influence or relegated its Christian citizens to their proper place: their own home and their own church.

September 11 changed America less than we think, and it did not change the law at all. This book presents a few, simple propositions:

Evangelical Christians and cultural liberals both believe fundamentally incompatible worldviews, and both groups hold these views with religious intensity; but only one is permitted to use the immense power and influence of government to teach its morality and, ultimately, change the heart of a nation.

Through the use of real-life examples and case studies, I will demonstrate how the liberal worldview can be legally "preached" from public school classrooms, college orientation sessions, and mandatory workplace seminars and workshops. I will show how the law will give a cultural liberal every right to speak—regardless of the forum and setting—but shut off even the private workplace from Christian expression. I will show how the law allows the government to force Christians (and Christian children) to hear a moral message that is fundamentally opposed to clear, biblical commands and principles yet often refuses to allow Christian teachers or employers to offer even a glimpse at a faith-based alternative.

In other words, our government—a government founded and formed by men of faith—is not a neutral player in the culture war. While Congress, the Supreme Court, and the president may or may not be opposed to Christians, they have together, over many years, created a comprehensive legal structure that is biased *against* faith.

It is only after we understand this fundamental legal truth that we can begin to formulate a response. We must understand the overall context of arguments for and against school prayer, for and against public school Bible clubs, and for and against religious harassment guidelines *before* we take strong public stands on vital issues of the day.

My ultimate conclusions in this book may surprise or even disturb you. Unlike many Christians, I do not seek to reverse the playing field and bias government in favor of faith. We evangelical Christians must realize that, as a minority in a democratic country, the faith our government would choose to support would not necessarily be the faith we support. As you fight for public school prayer, ask yourself, "If I win, to whom will they pray—and for what?" If you think honestly about the issue, you may not like the answer.

The ultimate solution to the unbalanced playing field is not bias in our favor but true neutrality. Politically, Christians should seek freedom—nothing more and most certainly nothing less. If we truly have confidence in our message, if we truly believe that our words are guided and inspired by the Holy Spirit of God, then we do not need government coercion or government endorsement to persuade millions to embrace Christ. We need only the freedom to speak.

In the pages that follow, you will read stories that will shock and outrage you. You will see the real-life consequences of a legal system that allows the government to teach a morality that is opposed to Christ, and you will see the potential for even further injustice and coercion. You will see the hatred of the opposition and the religious zeal of their words and actions. These stories—taken from my own life and from the real-life cases of embattled Christians around the country—demonstrate conclusively the extent to which secular liberals may not only use the law to require Christians to listen to their message but also to restrain Christians from offering a contrary view. These stories illustrate the extent to which true religious freedom—a freedom specifically enshrined by the United States Constitution—is diminishing in our schools and in our workplaces.

However, amidst the coercion and imbalance lie seeds of hope. As the cultural left oppresses and silences Christians, it often overplays its hand. Christian America—so often portrayed as overbearing and moralizing—finds that it is now fighting for that most fundamental of American values: freedom. In the aftermath of September 11, freedom is the one American value that is most often contrasted with the values of the Taliban's Afghanistan or Saddam Hussein's Iraq. Thanks to the oppression of the left, American Christians face a historic opportunity. As America becomes focused anew on questions of law and religion, we can stake new moral ground by standing firmly for religious freedom and against governmental moral coercion. With confidence in the eternal strength of our message, we can fight for neutral legal structures that allow *all* religious voices to be heard and permit the government to favor no one worldview. Now is the time to remind America who it really is and what it really stands for. Perhaps the pain and soul-searching caused by the most devastating day in American history can bring the advent of a new season in America: a season for freedom—a season for justice.

1

Becoming a Culture Warrior

I had never seen teenagers so on fire for God.

Only a week before, my wife and I had been living in New York City. I was slaving away in a large law firm, working seventy and eighty hours a week on multimillion-dollar commercial lawsuits, while my wife Nancy lived the life, as she called it, of a "well-financed single person." She shopped at Macy's by herself, went to Broadway plays by herself, and attended church, usually by herself. It was only our first year in New York, but the situation was quickly becoming intolerable. We had to leave.

The decision to leave was easy, but knowing where to go was difficult. Nancy initially thought Los Angeles would be exciting, primarily because she had grown accustomed to New York's shopping options and knew that L.A. stores rivaled the Big Apple's. I advocated Denver. I knew the pace there was slower, and I love to ski.

Faced with a decisional impasse, we did what we should have done from the beginning—we turned to God. After praying, sharing our insights, and praying even more, the answer became clear. It was Christmas of 1996 when we realized that the stores on Rodeo Drive and the ski slopes of Colorado would be left unscathed. Instead, we packed up and headed south to my hometown of Georgetown, Kentucky. This decision was so averse to our natural inclinations that we knew God must have had a purpose for the decision. And we were right.

Georgetown was where we saw the teenagers. It was the first weekend in March 1997, and Nancy and I were standing next to my parents, anxious about our first visit to a new church. Trinity Assembly of God in Georgetown was allegedly in the midst of a revival. My parents were youth sponsors for the church youth group and told us amazing stories about teens being saved every week, causing the youth group to grow (in a small church of around three hundred members) from thirty teens to more than eighty. More than anything else, they told us of the kids' incredible zeal for God.

I was skeptical. I knew teenagers. I had been one only nine years before, and I remembered what "zeal" meant to me. Zeal meant church attendance, abstinence, and no dates. Zeal meant being occasionally moved by a devotional song. Zeal did not mean any real, palpable joy in church, and it certainly did not mean effective evangelism.

My skepticism was undiminished when, at the beginning of that first visit, the church's pastor asked the congregation to stand so that the teens could come into the sanctuary "and pray for the adults." I smirked. *I wonder whose brilliant idea that is,* I thought. *Probably a youth pastor simply trying to impress, trying to whip up some fervor in his too-cool-for-words flock.*

What happened next shook me to my core. I heard some noise in the back of the church and turned to see an amazing sight. Dozens of kids, many of them weeping, some of them trembling violently, were streaming into the sanctuary. They took their stations at the end of each pew and, with outstretched arms and pleading faces, asked each adult if they needed prayer. Within seconds, dozens of adults left their seats and embraced these kids, begging for just a small slice of the joy, hope, and redemption these teenagers were so obviously feeling. The air was thick with emotion and a real sense of the presence of God.

My mind was reeling. I had never in my entire churchgoing life seen devotion that extreme and emotion that intense. *Why don't I feel that? Could I ever feel that way?* We stayed long after church was over. We talked to the pastor and to my parents. This time we listened without the filter of skepticism and disbelief.

Trinity Assembly of God had a passion for youth ministry. Stanley Holder, the pastor of this small church, had a vision that one day two hundred young people would worship together at Trinity. Pursuing that vision, the church had poured its resources into reaching the community's children. The goal was not to siphon other church kids from less dynamic youth ministries into Trinity's fun and contemporary worship. Instead, the goal was to reach those who never went to church, those who were lost in the abyss of drugs, alcohol, and hopeless sexuality.

Trinity succeeded beyond its wildest dreams. By mid-1996, it was clear that the small church's sanctuary and classrooms were simply not adequate to meet the demands of a growing ministry. Sometimes sixty or more teenagers would pack into a small, sweaty classroom, eagerly soaking up the Word. As teens were set free from the chains of sin, news began to spread, and even more kids began to come. Not waiting on invitations or evangelism, Georgetown's teenagers were filling every available space, and by the late fall, there was literally no more room at the inn. Something had to be done.

The answer was the Spirit Life Center, a multipurpose building that served as Sunday school building, worship hall, and activities center for the growing youth ministry. The Spirit Life Center was not fancy or even particularly expensive by the standards of most churches, but it strained Trinity's financial resources to their limit. Trinity is no suburban megachurch. Its members, though hardly poverty stricken, were not the collection of doctors, lawyers, accountants, and entrepreneurs that populate so many of America's affluent, evangelical congregations. Trinity is a hardworking, blue-collar church. Many of the members gave well beyond their tithes, and many of them supplemented their financial gifts with invaluable sweat equity.

In January 1997 the Spirit Life Center opened, and it was an immediate success. By late February, Wednesday night youth worship services were averaging more than eighty teens, and more than twenty kids had given their lives to Christ in that month alone. In March, attendance topped ninety. In the local high school, other kids joked that Trinity "ran" the school and marveled that one youth group could draw members of virtually every social clique in the county. Cheerleaders and baseball players worshiped next to farm boys and science fiction geeks. Even the formerly impenetrable color barrier began to crack as the Spirit Life Center welcomed African-American worshipers and speakers.

Although Nancy and I were fascinated and blessed by the youth revival, we also were confused. We clearly felt God's call to come to this town—to this very church—yet there seemed to be no need for a lawyer in the midst of such an outpouring. Never before had I seen a ministry so successful, so complete.

Then came the telephone call. It was late March 1997, and I was sitting at my desk in my new law firm, working on yet another allegedly "significant" piece of commercial litigation, when my secretary told me that my pastor was on the phone. I was a little surprised. He had never called me at work.

"Hey, Pastor. What's going on?" As I talked, I flipped through some deposition transcripts.

"We might have a problem."

"What is it?"

"Well, I really don't think it's that big a deal, but I wanted to call a lawyer, and you're the only one at the church."

I laughed inwardly. *Being the only option is hardly a ringing endorsement.*

The pastor continued. "You know our neighbors, the Smiths [not their real names], don't you?"

I knew the Smiths. They lived in the only home near Trinity, a large house located about fifty yards from the Spirit Life Center. A line of trees and a fence separated the church from the Smiths' property, but they were still relatively close. "Yeah, I had Mrs. Smith in eighth-grade English . . . a good teacher."

"That's what I hear. Anyway, they've always been opposed to having a church next to their property. They were against our church when it was first built, and they opposed the Spirit Life Center. Because they complained, the county required us to build that fence at the church. I don't think they wanted to have to look at our new building."

"OK."

"Well, Mr. Smith has been calling lately, complaining that they can hear the worship music from the Spirit Life Center. He says it's so loud that it rattles his windows. In fact, he says he's complained to the Board of Adjustments, and there's a hearing scheduled for next month."

"So loud it rattles his windows? Is that true? I've never noticed anything, and I've been outside while the youth are worshiping."

"I think he's exaggerating, but I really want to be a good neighbor. I've decided to station some church members outside during youth worship. If they can hear the music while standing next to his property, then they're supposed to go into the Spirit Life Center and tell them to turn the music down. I'm writing Mr. Smith a letter telling him this, but I'd like for you to look at it first, if you don't mind. Also, I might need you to call him. I really don't think that this will be a big deal, but I just felt that I needed to get you involved."

I had no idea at the time, but that telephone call changed the course of my life. A chain of events unfolded that eventually resulted in my representing not only my own church but several other embattled churches, denominational organizations, ministry groups, and individual Christians. Within months I was interviewed by newspapers, magazines, and television stations as the lawyer for a courageous church. Within two years I (temporarily) quit the commercial practice of law entirely and devoted myself to teaching, writing, and the continued representation of Christians. Within three years I was invited to speak at nationally significant symposiums as an advocate for religious freedom in the face of coercive political correctness.

But all of that was a long way off in March 1997. At the time I thought that the pastor's call meant a meeting with the Smiths, possibly a letter or two, or, at most, a brief appearance before the zoning board. I couldn't have been more wrong. The story of what followed is interesting not only because of its own drama, pathos, and anguish, but also because it is one example of the challenges faced by countless Christians in a nation that can no longer be called Christian. It is an example of the new persecution—a persecution that comes not from the Supreme Court, Congress, or the president, but from your friends, neighbors, and employers, your local school boards, zoning boards, and colleges.

It is persecution at the grass roots.

"No Sound Whatsoever"

Needless to say, Mr. Smith was not placated by the pastor's letter. Nor was he satisfied when we took sound readings and found that the sound level of the music at the property line was lower than the sound levels of crickets chirping and the wind blowing through the trees. Nor was he satisfied when we went to his home, apologized for the inconvenience and irritation, turned the sound so low it could not be heard at all in his home (even with the windows open), and fixed the master volume controls so they could not possibly be turned up above the approved level. Mr. Smith wanted his day before the zoning board. He vowed that he would "shut us down."

Even then I was not worried. The local zoning board was comprised of political appointees. The county's highest elected official selected the board, who served multiyear terms. He was known to be a good man, and several members of the board were reported to be "churchgoing folk." Those political appointees were facing a complaint against a church that had bent over backward to accommodate its neighbors' concerns. Two voters were challenging several hundred. Political mathematics alone dictated the outcome.

Not only was fairness and mathematics on our side, but the law was as well. The church was in full compliance with each and every requirement of its conditional use permit. Additionally, the county did not even have a noise ordinance on its books. I had vivid childhood memories of lying in bed and hearing "tractor pulls" rattle my bedroom windows from almost two miles away. (Ironically, those tractor pulls took place within a quarter mile of the Smith home. Yet, to our knowledge, there had never been any complaint.) Simply put, the board had no legal basis to act against the church.

Finally, the church was being represented by a Harvard-trained attorney. Experience had not yet taught me real humility, so I imagined that the board would be quite impressed by their hometown-boy-made-good. I imagined that they had rarely seen such a well-educated, eloquent attorney before this simple, rural county board. I truly believed that my presence alone would be decisive.

The meeting started well enough. Approximately two hundred church members were present, including fifty teens from the youth group. The pastor and individual church members spoke, describing all of the things that the church had done in response to Mr. Smith's complaint. I spoke and described the legal framework. But the real highlight of the meeting was provided by the teenagers. Several of them gave profoundly moving accounts of how their lives had been changed by the Trinity youth ministry. One young woman described her previous life in witchcraft; others described lives full of alcohol, violence, and hopelessness. One teenager brought down the house when he stood up, surveyed the court-like surroundings of the meeting room, and declared, "I always knew I'd end up in court; I just thought it'd be as a criminal." I concluded Trinity's case by asking the board not to impose an illegal "cone of silence" on a congregation that was doing so much good. It was a powerful presentation.

The Smiths spoke next. They distorted the facts, took statements out of context, and spoke with much anger and passion. They attacked me, the pastor, the youth pastor, and even my father. It was terrible to endure, and it became even more uncomfortable when I noticed that several members of the board were nodding throughout Mr. Smith's speech, often glaring at the pastor and at me.

When Mr. Smith finished, I rose to rebut his statements but was cut short. "It's late," said the chairman, "and before the meeting, I promised Mrs. Smith that this wouldn't take long." He smiled at her. It was then that I knew we were doomed.

The board deliberated, in a huddle, for no longer than four minutes. The verdict was delivered: Trinity was ordered to adjust its use of the Spirit Life Center so that "no sound whatsoever" could escape its walls. To enforce the board's order, the county building inspector was told to monitor Trinity's use of the building. If the board's orders were violated, he was to padlock its doors shut. If Trinity wanted to continue to use the Spirit Life Center, the board explained, it would have to be completely soundproofed.

We were stunned. The order was so draconian, it was impossible to comply. Even if the teens sang without the accompaniment of instruments, the sound of their singing would drift out the buildings' windows or through a door as it swung open and shut. The bouncing of a basketball caused faint noise outside the center. Under the literal terms of the board's order, any sound that escaped the building was illegal, even if that noise did not reach neighboring properties. The implication was clear: the Spirit Life Center, a $300,000 building and the cornerstone of Trinity's youth outreach efforts, had to be shut down.

I cannot recall a more humiliating, devastating moment in my career. I had let the pastor down. I had let the church down. Most importantly, I had let the teens down—the very ones who had given me more hope and spiritual inspiration than they would ever know.

The days and weeks that followed were even worse. With inadequate seating and facilities, attendance at youth worship plummeted, and the teens were demoralized. Many parents in the community refused to allow their children to attend Trinity, convinced that the church had to be doing something wrong for the board to react so strongly. I felt so much shame that I could hardly even look at the pastor or any of the other congregants.

Ten days after the board's decision, the pastor invited me to meet with the church's deacons. We met on a Wednesday night, after a particularly dispiriting youth worship service. The pastor began the meeting by looking directly at me and asking, simply and abruptly, "What can we do to change this?"

I felt the deacons' eyes on me, the newcomer to their church, the legal captain who had just driven the ship straight into an iceberg. Flushed with embarrassment, I answered the question as honestly as I could. "I think our only option is to file a lawsuit. I've looked at the law, and the only way to appeal their ruling is through the court. We don't have an opportunity to ask the board to reconsider. Even if we did, you saw their faces—they enjoyed ruling against us. We're not getting anywhere with that board. We can either file a lawsuit or live with the decision."

I could see some of the deacons cringe. Churches are not and should not be in the litigation business, and I knew that they had no desire to become plaintiffs. I could see that other deacons had their jaws set. They wanted to fight. But before they fought, they wanted to know their chances. One spoke up. "Would we win?"

"I don't know. The law is on our side, and we've done all the right things. But the courts of this country are man's court, not God's, and injustice happens all the time. I don't know if any of you have ever been involved in lawsuits, but I can tell you that they're not pretty. They sometimes take years, they can be bitter, and I can almost promise the other side will do everything it can to make this church look unreasonable, dishonest, and unchristian. I'm not telling you not to do it, and I will take the case if you want me, but I do want to tell you what to expect."

There was a long silence. Each man was sobered by the decision before him, and each man, I could tell, wanted only to do God's will. The pastor spoke next.

"Ever since the meeting last Monday, I've been praying and studying Scripture. At first, I didn't really even consider a lawsuit or challenging this in any confrontational way, but then I remembered Paul. When he was being beaten by Roman soldiers, he stopped the beating by asserting his rights as a Roman citizen. That assertion set in motion an appeal process that took him all the way to Rome, and Paul used those years not only to write much of the New Testament but also to witness to every judge he appeared before. I believe God is calling us to stop this legal beating, and we'll appeal all the way to Rome if we have to."

The pastor took a breath. I saw heads nodding around the room.

"But that's not all we should do. We have an obligation, as ministers of the gospel, as Christians, to love our neighbor—to do everything we can to make this right with the Smiths. We're fighting the government's decision, not the Smiths, so I want us to soundproof that building. I know it's not really possible to make it completely soundproof, but we can do better, and we will. I don't care what it costs. It is the right thing to do, and we should do this—regardless of what you think about a lawsuit."

It was at that moment that the decision was truly made, although no vote was taken until several days later. It was at that moment that the pastor beautifully and courageously stated what Christians in adversity should do—fight injustice but love people.

While the church board deliberated, the senior partner of my law office, an honorable and decent man, allowed me to represent the church *pro bono,* for free. With his blessing I was able to devote several days and nights to drafting a complaint, writing briefs, and preparing motions. When the deacons finally made their decision, I would be ready. And this time there would be no overconfidence. This time I would throw myself on God's grace, not my own education or abilities.

Four days later, on Sunday night, the board made its decision. The next afternoon Trinity Assembly of God filed a complaint in the United States District Court for the Eastern District of Kentucky against the Scott County, Kentucky, Board of Adjustments. The battle was joined.

"We Can and Will Define How You Worship"

Less than a day later, I received my first telephone call from the media. Apparently, the local newspapers frequently reviewed case filings, hoping to find something interesting to report, and this case qualified. The reporter was polite and inquisitive, and by the end of the conversation, I truly believed that she was sympathetic to our cause.

The next morning's newspaper confirmed my hopes. A front-page article described Trinity's dilemma and accurately stated our position. The county refused to comment, leaving our story the only one available to the public. I was more than pleased. One of my greatest fears was that Trinity would be perceived by the public as litigious or arrogant for filing its suit. So far, so good.

Over the next few days, the media calls came pouring in. Most of the local television stations did reports from Trinity, and all of the area newspapers carried accurate, sympathetic articles. In the months that followed, newspapers nationwide would report on what was going on in our small church. Wary of the "liberal media," I was enormously gratified by its response.

Unfortunately, the media coverage was a two-edged sword. The negative publicity caused the county to dig in its heels. In the first court appearance of the lawsuit, the county's attorneys claimed our account of the board hearing was flawed and even produced draft hearing "minutes" that purported to show what "really" happened. They claimed our suit was utterly without merit and should be dismissed. Fortunately for us, the judge was not convinced by the county's arguments and urged it to agree to allow Trinity to reopen the Spirit Life Center while the suit was pending. Within ten days after the suit was filed, the Trinity youth group was praising God once more.

However, spiritual battles are not won so easily. In fact, the battle had just begun. Three times in the first two weeks after services resumed, youth worship was interrupted by visits from the police—acting in complete defiance of the judge's order. Each time, they firmly asked that we "turn the music down." Each time, the youth complied with police requests and resumed worship as best they could. An atmosphere of fear and intimidation pervaded youth services.

Events soon took a turn for the worse. While Trinity's leaders debated their response to the sheriff's harassment, I went back to the

Board of Adjustment, hoping to describe to the board members the extent of our comprehensive soundproofing work. I was allowed to speak at the end of their monthly meeting. They sat, stone-faced, while I detailed the thousands of dollars that Trinity was spending and outlined the progress of the work so far. I was not expecting a warm reception, but I must admit that I was utterly unprepared for what happened next.

At the conclusion of my remarks, one of the board members (I will call her Ms. Collins) grabbed the microphone. "Mr. French," she said, "before you sit down, I want to say a few things to you." She was scowling.

"Certainly." I had promised myself that I would be courteous no matter what happened in the meeting, and I would not allow her spite to disturb my calm.

"I've read the newspapers, and I want you to stop lying about me and this board."

"Ms. Collins, I never—"

She cut me off. "I read what you said, and you can't defend it. I'm doing the talking right now, and you're going to listen. I know you have a federal judge on this case, but I don't care. I don't care what any court says, your church is going to have to do what we say."

"But . . ."

My attempt to interrupt only inflamed her. "You know, what burns me is that you people pretend to be godly, but I think maybe you need to spend more time on your knees and less time making music. If you had, none of this would have happened."

When she took a breath, I was able to utter a quick response. "Ms. Collins, with all due respect, this board cannot define how we worship God."

Her response was quick and chilling. "We can and will define how you worship."

The meeting ended almost immediately after Ms. Collins's final statement. I remember walking outside with my head swimming. *These people hate us,* I thought. *Only complete and total victory will free us from their control. We must win this case.* The next Wednesday I reported Ms. Collins's statements to the rest of the church. Some church members were shocked and saddened, others were outraged, but each of them came to the same conclusion that I did. We had to win.

A Condescending Laugh

Litigation is all about details. When most people think of a court case, they think of dramatic moments in a packed courtroom. Stirring music plays as the lawyer delivers a soliloquy that drives the entire room to tears. The reality of litigation is much different. Court appearances are rare, and when they do happen, they are often before bored judges and indifferent juries. There is no music, and few, if any, tears. The reality of litigation is paperwork and mind-numbing tedium. Eyes tear up, not from emotion, but from exhaustion as lawyers burn the midnight oil reading thousands of pages of statutes, regulations, cases, memoranda, letters, and depositions, each page more stultifying than the last.

The Trinity case was no different. Not only did I have to wade through stacks of county files regarding its zoning practices, but I also had to spend days and weeks staring at dozens of different legal documents. There were county laws to decipher and comprehensive zoning regulations to understand, always within the context of a complex layer of constitutional law. I knew we had a strong case, but strong cases do not always win. Judges sometimes do not understand the law, and sometimes they will find ways to disregard your arguments if they disagree with your ideology. For victory to be assured (if it ever could be), I had to find a clear, simple, and unavoidable argument. I had to find the trump card.

In the late spring of 1998, while cross-referencing county zoning regulations with deposition transcripts, I found the answer. I discovered that in Scott County, Kentucky, churches were the only organization that did not have an absolute right to locate at least somewhere in the county. For a church to exist, it had to get prior approval from the Board of Adjustment. Schools could locate in certain zoning districts without prior board approval. So could theaters. So could secular auditoriums or gymnasiums. But not churches. Churches had to come, hat in hand, to the board and seek permission to worship. Not only was this discrimination outrageous, but it was also clearly and unequivocally against the law.

As quickly as I could, I prepared a motion that asked the court to invalidate the Scott County zoning ordinance on the ground that it discriminated on the basis of religion. The county's response was brief. In essence, they argued that the Constitution gave them the discretion to discriminate in purely local matters. They also argued that the requirement that churches (and churches alone) seek prior approval before operating was not discriminatory. When I read their response, I knew they had lost—if the judge was paying attention.

My motion was filed in May. Three months later, one hot, August afternoon, I received a telephone call from the county's lawyer. He asked me if Trinity wanted to settle the case before it went to trial. I told him that we might be interested, but only if we could agree that the county would not shut down the Spirit Life Center and would not interfere with the operation of the church. His response was quick.

"I'm not sure that we can ever agree to that. I think that we can only agree to allow your operation if the soundproofing is acceptable."

My response was equally quick. "There's no way we'll settle under those terms. Acceptable according to whose standard? The Smiths? Ms. Collins? I know what they think of us, and we just can't be placed under their thumb."

"You might want to rethink. We're going to trial soon, and if you lose . . ." He did not finish the sentence. We both knew what would happen if the church lost. The Spirit Life Center would be closed, and the church would be permanently placed at the mercy of a hostile, vindictive zoning board.

"I don't think we're going to trial. We filed our motion, and the judge will rule soon—"

I was cut off by a condescending laugh. "I really don't think you'll win your motion. We'll talk again after the judge denies your request." He hung up.

The very next afternoon, on 17 August 1998, the judge ruled in our favor. The Scott County zoning ordinance was invalidated, and Trinity Assembly of God (and every other church in the county) was freed from the tyranny of the Board of Adjustment.

I will never forget that night. I was late for church and walked in to the sanctuary still wearing my work "uniform," a navy suit and yellow tie. I clutched the judge's opinion in my left hand. At Trinity, it was customary for individuals, during lulls in worship, to stand and give a testimony about God's work in their lives during the past week. At the earliest opportunity, I stood up.

"Pastor, I have something to say."

"Go ahead, David." He looked puzzled.

I walked up to the front of the church and, with shaking hands, turned to the first page of the judge's opinion. "You all remember what happened last April—how we felt that night, when the Spirit Life Center was shut down and our youth ministry was placed in danger. You remember the police visits and the threats against us. Even yesterday, I got a call from the county's lawyer, and he didn't have much good to say. He told us that we would lose this case, and we all know what that would mean." I paused to catch my breath. I glanced up at the congregation. Every eye was glued to the paper I held in my hand.

"Well, a couple of hours ago, I received this piece of paper from the federal court, and this piece of paper officially invalidates the Scott County zoning ordinance and frees this and every church from the control of the Board of Adjustment." I could see the pastor's wife begin to cry. Tears rolled down my cheeks. "We won."

The entire congregation lifted their voices in praise to God. Teenagers and adults wept with joy. I could hardly contain myself. My mind raced back through the humiliations and tribulations of the last eighteen months, and I was overcome with gratitude to God that he had delivered victory. I was overcome that he had given a cocky young lawyer a second chance. Trinity sought and obtained justice, but for me, it was more than justice. In that small town, and in that small church, I received grace.

Fighting the Good Fight

Something else happened to me during that experience. I became, for better or worse, what the media might call a "culture warrior." I am not a person who argues national policy on late-night television, or even a person who demonstrates for or against the cause of the moment. Instead, I have fought small battles in small places—battles to keep the gospel alive in America. I have tried (and sometimes failed) to save churches and ministry groups from extinction. I have tried to make sure that, at the very least, Christians can speak the love of God in a country that often cares little for that love or for God's people.

During those battles, and during my time in the academic environment, I have seen things that have caused me great concern. I have seen academics debating policy changes that could destroy religious freedom in private universities and corporations—institutions that are of critical importance to almost all of us. I have seen local governments enact zoning ordinances and regulations that leave church ministries crippled and pastors baffled, and I have seen Christian student groups declared dangerous and banned from elite college campuses.

I have seen some other disturbing things, but these wrongs come from some of our own brothers and sisters. I have seen Christians with chips on their shoulders, so focused on vindicating their "rights" that they forget the gospel. I have seen Christians fight the wrong battles at the wrong time, leaving us vulnerable to mockery and moral defeat by our "enemies." And I have seen Christians forget they are seeking justice and instead attack individuals, inflicting pain merely because pain was inflicted on them.

This book is designed to give Christians a new view of the legal culture war—one that exposes the atrocities on both sides of the battle. In the following pages, I will reveal some of the strategies of the opposition and use their own words to describe their goals in the struggle. I also will reveal the real source of legal persecution, the actual individuals and organizations that will impact your lives. The persecution that you may experience typically does not come from the president, the Congress, or the Supreme Court—from the institutions politically minded Christians focus on the most—but from your local city council, zoning board, and public school district. It comes from your employer, your friends, and your neighbors. Most ominously, it sometimes comes from your fellow Christians.

Again and again, as I see the same battles fought over much of the same ground, I go back to the example of Paul. He understood there was a purpose behind his legal stand. His purpose was not the vindication of his rights, but instead, the spread of the good news. If vindication of rights were our highest goal, Jesus would have resisted unjust punishment at the cross. The culture war should be fought, not to impose our will or to protect our turf, but to ensure that this generation and the next can hear the words of Jesus and receive his grace. The legal culture war is not about legislating a Christian nation into existence. It is not about commandments on school walls, slogans on courthouses, deistic graduation prayers, or nativity scenes in public parks. It is about preserving, for every person in this country, access to the gospel message—the message that calls them to humble themselves, take up their cross, and follow Christ. Only the cumulative effect of millions of those wonderful, free choices will create the nation we say we want. Only the cumulative effect of denying that choice to millions will truly destroy the nation we say we love.

2

Understanding
the Battle

The Religion That's Safe
for Government

"He is an antichrist, a Hitler, and it's like having a serial murderer debate the value of life."[1] With these words a prominent Hawaii lawyer launched a frontal attack on one of the most hated individuals in America—a man so hated that the very possibility he would be invited to address a public gathering caused a call for an "affirmative action investigation" into the "racial sensitivity" of the invitation. Others echoed the battle cry: "I didn't want to invite him, and I still don't. If not Hitler, he is a Goebbels." "He is an intellectual fraud."

Who was this terrible individual? What kind of man was so hated that a group of lawyers—of civil libertarians—did not even want him in their presence? The answer may surprise you. These attacks were not directed at noted racist politician David Duke, nor were they directed at an actual murderer like Timothy McVeigh. No, this "Hitler," this

27

"antichrist" was Clarence Thomas, Associate Justice of the Supreme Court of the United States. What precipitated the Hawaii ACLU's outrage was the decision of a local subcommittee to invite Justice Thomas to debate noted liberal civil libertarian and scholar Nadine Strossen at an annual First Amendment conference.

The stated purpose of the conference was to offer "spirited" debate on various constitutional issues, and the subcommittee that first issued the invitation thought Clarence Thomas—like previous conservative participants Justice Antonin Scalia and former Christian Coalition leader Ralph Reed—would be an excellent choice to offer a counterpoint to Ms. Strossen's admittedly liberal views on affirmative action and civil rights. How wrong they were. In the words of one of the complaining attorneys, "Bringing Clarence Thomas sends a message that the Hawaii ACLU promotes and honors black Uncle Toms who turn their backs on civil rights." The ACLU board heard these complaints and voted 12–3 against inviting Thomas. After this demonstration of sufficient racial sensitivity, the "affirmative action complaint" against the Hawaii ACLU was withdrawn. Clarence Thomas was put in his place.

There was a time when I would have been shocked by this news item, stunned at the disrespect directed at a justice of the Supreme Court and amazed that any individual thought he or she could get away with such grotesque distortions and slander. How, precisely, was Clarence Thomas like Hitler? How many millions of innocents has Justice Thomas killed? How was he even a Goebbels—a key policy maker in a Fascist death machine? Could these people be serious? Do they even believe what they are saying? I once would have found it difficult to believe that any rational individual actually thought these things and even more difficult to believe that their prejudice and ignorance would receive a hearing in the state office of a respected legal organization.

I am no longer shocked or even surprised. And yes, I have found that supposedly rational individuals *do* believe what they are saying when they make such wild accusations. With all their heart, they believe they are fighting evil in America, fending off the forces of darkness who seek to oppress minorities, subjugate women, and throw gays into the pits of despair. To these righteous individuals, social conservatives like Clarence Thomas—especially Christian social conservatives— are the mortal enemy. To them, our views and attempts to "impose morality" represent the greatest threat to enlightened society and good government. The answer to our zeal is greater zeal—directed against the enemies of tolerance.

A Memorable Conversation

I'll never forget the moment I first realized the magnitude of feeling behind the liberal left's seemingly outrageous words. It was during one of those endless, late-night conversations that characterize the law school experience. A conversation that had begun in class was spilling over into dinner. My classmate was a gay man, about ten years older than I, and—like many of my classmates—passionately concerned about social justice. I was fresh out of David Lipscomb University, one of the more conservative Christian schools in the country. He was from Berkeley, home of the anything-goes free speech movement. My undergrad school featured curfews of 11:00 P.M. on weeknights and midnight on weekends. He found the very idea of a curfew both retrograde and repressive. My dormitory had housed men only—women weren't allowed beyond the lobby. His dorm had been coed—including the showers. At Lipscomb, you could be suspended or expelled for engaging in premarital sex. At Berkeley, he related, sex and explorations of sexuality were seen as integral elements of the educational experience.

I could tell that he found me strange. I was so far outside the realm of his normal experience that I might as well have landed on Harvard Square from the planet Mars. I was the kind of person that his professors railed against, that his classmates hissed, and that he himself mocked—just moments before—during discussions of public policy and morality. He told me he had never actually met a "member of the religious right." He also told me he had never, in his entire educational life, heard religiously conservative arguments from someone who actually believed them. I felt like a specimen on a petri dish.

Sometimes it is difficult for religious conservatives to realize the truth that we are—undeniably—a minority. Many of us don't have a single friend that is not Christian, and we live in areas of the country that pride themselves on church attendance and religious affiliation. Even if we can't begin high school football games with prayer, we still begin Chamber of Commerce and Rotary Club meetings with invocations. We're shocked when we meet someone who really, truly does not believe in God, and we feel comfortable, in most social settings, openly lamenting the immorality of our modern culture.

I know that's how I grew up. My family went to church three times a week, and I spent another night or two at youth group functions or with youth group friends. Although my public high school was rife with all the worst problems of modern American public education, my close friends were well outside the sex-drugs-alcohol party circle. I don't recall a single debate about gay rights during high school, and I certainly never encountered a real debate in college—where you could be expelled for homosexual behavior.

We had just left a class where the topic of discussion had been rather mundane—statutory interpretation. During the class discussion, I mentioned that one should try to understand what laws mean by reading the words and applying the plain language of the statute. When the professor pointed out that sometimes the "plain language" is confusing or ambiguous, I said that confusion or ambiguity should cause us to investigate the original intent of the drafter. What did they intend to mean when this law was written? What were they trying to accomplish? To me, the entire issue seemed rather simple—just do what the law says.

Much to my surprise, that view was met with condescension and chuckles. My classmates called me naive, misguided, or malicious. I was instantly branded as a conservative. My classmates generally embraced the opinion of my professor—that language was almost infinitely malleable, and it should be molded to achieve the "just" result. In his words, "First, you decide what is right. Then, after you're sure of the result, argue that the language of the statute—whatever that language is—compels that just result." To my professor, language was simply a tool. Words had no meaning other than the one you assigned them. Consequently, the law was meaningless unless *you* gave it meaning—and that meaning had to be consistent with social justice.

I found the class discussion exhilarating and frustrating. It was exhilarating to stand more or less alone in front of dozens of intelligent opponents, fighting the lonely battle for truth and objectivity. It was frustrating to see that no one seemed to listen to anything I said. Instead, they tripped over themselves in their eagerness to condemn me and my obviously right-wing or extremist point of view.

The class argument (it was not really a discussion) spilled over into the halls after class and continued as I walked back toward my dormitory. By the time I'd reached the first restaurant off campus, only one person was still with me. I invited him to join me for dinner. After some preliminary small talk and mutual complaints about the food, we got back to business.

"So, David, do you think of yourself as a member of the religious right?"

I thought a moment before replying, hesitant to brand myself in a way that might cause him to ignore my ideas. "Well, I don't know. I'm

Christian—I guess you'd call me a fundamentalist Christian, and I'm conservative—pro-life and all that, so . . . yeah, sure. I'm in the religious right."

"Really?" He seemed surprised that I'd admit such a thing. "So you voted for Pat Robertson, and you actually agree with Jerry Falwell."

"No, and not always. To be honest, I don't really know all the things they stand for, particularly when it comes to foreign policy, economics . . . things like that. But, overall, I do like them."

He stifled a smile, a friendly smile. "Honestly, you're the first person I've ever met who admitted to that. Amazing." But the smile soon faded. "I want to ask you a question—a question I've always wanted to ask a conservative Christian. You're against gay rights, right?"

I started to get nervous. I knew he was gay, and I knew that I could easily offend him if I wasn't careful with my words. "Well, it depends on what you mean . . ."

He cut me off. "Yeah, yeah. Let's make it simple. Would you want a gay man to be your son's kindergarten teacher?"

My answer was quick. "No."

"Why not?"

"Let me clarify. I wouldn't fear that a gay man would molest my son, nor do I think a gay man is less qualified to teach reading, math, or any other academic subject."

"Then why wouldn't you want him to teach your son?"

"I want my son to have a Christian education, and most practicing gays don't share a lot of my values. Same goes for heterosexuals. A straight guy who's sleeping with his girlfriend or is having an affair on his wife wouldn't be any better."

"See, that's something that really bothers me. You know, I think you'd be amazed at how many values you share with many gay men. I bet if we talked long enough, we'd find a lot that we agreed on. What if your acceptable Christian is a bad teacher? Or cruel to the kids? You'd let him teach but not a talented gay teacher? Are you afraid he'd tell a five-year-old to have sex with men?"

I was feeling extremely uncomfortable. To be honest, I had never really thought about this issue—or most other issues regarding sexuality or sexual orientation. I essentially was starting from one premise: homosexual practice was wrong. Everything else was just shooting from the hip. "I don't think I'm really communicating well. Let me back up a minute and just lay my cards on the table. I can't talk specific policy without giving you my starting presumption, because, to be honest, I can tell I haven't thought about this as much as you . . ."

"So, without thinking, you decide gays can't teach your kids."

"I know that's what it sounds like, but you have to understand that my faith is everything to me. Everything. Jesus Christ's sacrifice on the cross is what gives my life meaning and purpose. To me, there is no greater gift in life than a relationship with Jesus, and there's no worse fate than separation from God. Jesus said that if we love Him, then we'll keep His commands, and the Bible contains commands regarding sexual practice. I love Jesus, so I try to keep those commands. So, when I say I don't want my son being taught by someone who doesn't share those values, it's because it breaks my heart to think that my son—when I have one—would choose to depart from those values. Now, I know it's highly unlikely that a kindergarten teacher would ever successfully persuade my child to defy Scripture and become gay—or that a teacher would even try—but I think that by understanding my background, you might understand why I gave you the answer I did. Jesus Christ is life—abundant life—and I want that for my son. I want that for everyone."

I could tell he was not quite prepared for my answer, and something about it deeply disturbed him. His response was solemn. "Why would you bind me with your chains?"

"What? But, Jesus doesn't . . ."

"Bind me? I don't know about Jesus, but your view of Him does. Do you want to know what I've seen?" His eyes were glistening with emotion. "Do you?"

"Sure. You've listened to me . . ."

"I've seen men weeping with despair at their loveless marriages, racked with guilt at their feelings, yet unable to change them. I've seen these men—respected businessmen, family men—reduced to cruising the dark alleyways of cities, looking to prostitutes to satisfy desires they can't control. Have you ever seen the anguish of a man forced by society, by people like you, to spend a lifetime denying his essential nature? I've seen it, and it's terrible. It wounds my heart. Let me tell you something: this is not a choice. I'll say it again. This is not a choice. I did not choose anything. I am who I am, and I can't believe that you would use a faith that I don't believe to deny me or one of my friends a job I might love and be good at."

This was not going well. I did not expect the intensity of his feelings, the passion with which he responded to me. I had opened up just a bit—hoping to introduce Christ into the conversation, hoping to begin the process of evangelizing him. In response, he had poured out his soul, not in a moment of redemptive clarity, but instead as part of a heartfelt effort to change my mind. He was evangelizing *me*.

My response was quiet and (hopefully) gentle. "You know . . ." I paused and took a breath. "There's another kind of anguish—another kind of pain. There's the pain of separation. We were created to know God and to love God. And when we turn away from that, we experience pain. Maybe not right away. Maybe not for years, but the pain comes. I know I'm not in your shoes, and I know I don't stand in the shoes of many people who struggle with things that I can't comprehend, but I believe—to the bottom of my heart—that it's only in Christ that anyone can find ultimate peace—not in relationships, not in careers, and not even in sex."

"Well, you're just wrong about that."

"How—"

". . . can I say that? I'm at peace with myself and I'm gay. I'm happy and I'm gay. I'm only unhappy when surrounded by people who try to tell me that there is something wrong with the essence of who I am. Guilt is inflicted. It doesn't occur naturally. And I still cannot understand, even after what you've told me, how you can use your faith to deny me anything."

Throughout the conversation both of us struggled to keep the conversation civil. My problem was not with anger but with nerves. I did not know if I was saying the right things in the right way. I wanted to communicate truth, but I also wanted that truth to be communicated with love. I could see that my friend was struggling with frustration and anger. A few times I noticed his fist clenching, and his voice grew steadily quieter, more intense. He truly could not fathom I would make a faith-based decision that, when carried into the realm of public policy or even private conduct, would impact him or someone he loved.

I thought for quite some time before I spoke again. To break the awkward silence, I slurped at my empty Coke and picked at the remaining crumbs of my sandwich. My mind was searching for the right way to communicate my ideas. Faith . . . faith seemed to be the key. He was offended by the idea that my personal faith could affect him.

I looked up from plate and blurted a response: "And I can't understand why you'd try to impose your faith upon me or, especially, my children."

"My faith?" He laughed.

"Yes. You believe homosexuality is an immutable personal characteristic, like skin color. That's unproven, so your conviction is—at some level—based on faith. You believe my beliefs regarding Jesus and the

Bible are flat wrong. Yet you've given me nothing that proves they're wrong, and I doubt you have that information. So that's another faith-based assumption. I could go on and on, but you get the point. Both of us, when you get right down to it, are acting on faith. That's not to say that we both don't have evidence to support our faith—I believe I have a lot of evidence to support the claims of Christ and the truth of the Bible—but it does mean we both make fundamental assumptions about life and eternity that we cannot prove to the other's satisfaction. That's faith."

"Yes, but the difference is, you want to practice your faith on me, while I simply want you to leave me alone. That's the critical difference."

"Well, not really. If you were a kindergarten teacher, and one of the kids in the class lived with lesbian parents and the other kids made fun of him, wouldn't you step in, stop the mocking and, possibly, explain that there was nothing wrong with the child's family relationship?"

He thought a moment before answering. "I probably would do just that. Or I might just ban teasing entirely and take that kid aside by himself and tell him that there was nothing wrong with his family. I might even tell him it's like my own family—or the family I hope to have someday. What would you do? Allow the mocking to continue? Not comfort the child who was teased?"

"I'm not sure what I'd do—definitely stop the teasing immediately and try to comfort the child in some way, maybe by spending extra time with him. I couldn't tell him it was just fine that parents lived that way, but I also wouldn't tell him it was wrong. Kids don't choose their parents. If I was in a public school, I'd be hesitant to try to indoctrinate the child in a particular way, possibly to drive a wedge between him and his family. But don't you see what you'd do if you told the teasing kids there was nothing at all wrong with lesbian families?"

"Introduce some tolerance into an abusive situation?"

"Well, that and teach the other children a faith-based moral value I don't share or believe to be true. If your child had me for a teacher, and I tried to tell him his family structure wasn't best and why, then you would have a legal claim against me and my school for violating separation of church and state. If you tell my son something utterly incompatible with my family's faith, then what's my recourse? My children are at your mercy. That's why I answered the way I did."

My friend laughed, breaking the tension. "At my mercy? I'm just wanting them to learn two plus two or maybe how to spell their names." He got up from the table. "Anyway, you're probably half the math teacher that I'd be."

I smiled. "Half? I'm twice the math teacher you are. Now, English, that's another matter. I did have only a Kentucky public school education . . ."

Thus ended a conversation that impacts me to this day. It started a process of discovery that colors how I watch television, how I read the newspapers, how I argue cases, and how I think about every issue of cultural significance. As evangelical Christians line up against gay rights advocates and invectives are hurled; as accusations of racism, sexism, and homophobia fill magazines, newspapers, cyberspace, and the airwaves; I don't see simple hatred of Christianity. The hatred is a byproduct of the fact that in so many significant areas we stand diametrically opposed to much of the liberal left. According to the tenets of their faith, Christians are the enemies of what is good and right. Christians are the enemies of "social justice." To us, cultural liberals are leading millions away from God—deceiving people into believing that fulfillment and peace can be found in racial identities, sexual expression, environmental communion, or in egalitarian notions of social interaction. Our faiths conflict. We cannot believe everything they say and still practice biblical Christianity. They cannot embrace our message without undergoing fundamental change. We are at an impasse.

Dueling Faiths

It's hardly original to state that the liberal left is essentially advancing a faith-based agenda. As will be discussed later in this book, Christians have been arguing for years that textbooks and schools have been preaching the religion of secular humanism. Other commentators have noted how various liberal ideas have their genesis in this or that religious tradition. However, what is relatively new—and to the evangelical Christian, extremely intimidating—is the extent to which the liberal left's ostensibly "political" agenda has become nothing short of an all-encompassing worldview.

In May 2001, Stanley Kurtz, a fellow at the Hudson Institute and regular commentator for *National Review,* wrote a fascinating article for the conservative magazine's online edition. Entitled "The Church of the Left," the article traced the evolution of liberalism from a political ideology that "laid out ground rules for reasoned debate and the peaceful adjudication of differences" to a pseudoreligion that "answers the big questions about life, lends significance to [liberals'] daily exertions, and provides a rationale for meaningful collective actions."[2]

Liberalism, arising as a reaction to the "destructive religious wars of Europe's past" was intended to allow people of "differing religious perspectives to live peacefully and productively in the same society." Because it was designed to "make the world safe for adherents of differing faiths, liberalism itself was never supposed to be a faith." To Kurtz, the key to understanding political correctness and much of today's vicious political dialogue is the realization that liberalism has departed from these benign roots and become a "de facto religion."

By understanding the religious intensity of liberal thought, we are able to understand why contemporary political discourse is laced with vicious attacks against conservatives. Politically conservative Christians who find themselves labeled "homophobic" for believing that gay sex is sinful, or "sexist" for believing in biblical marriage relationships, or "racist" for opposing affirmative action should understand precisely what is happening. Kurtz described the situation brilliantly:

> One of the main reasons why politics in a liberal society could be peaceful was that people sought direction about life's ultimate purpose outside of politics itself. But once traditional religion ceased to provide modern liberals with either an ultimate life purpose or a pattern of virtue, liberalism itself was the only belief system remaining that could supply these essential elements of life. . . . So long as [liberalism] serves as a mere set of ground rules for adjudicating day-to-day political differences, liberalism remains too "boring" to serve as a religion. But what if liberals were engaged at every moment in a dire, almost revolutionary, struggle for the very principles of liberalism itself? What if liberals were at war on a daily basis with King George III? With Hitler? With Bull Connor? Now that would supply a purpose to life—a purpose capable of endowing even our daily exertions with a larger significance, and certainly a collective purpose that would provide a rationale for meaningful collective action.[3]

A close observation of daily life proves the truth of Kurtz's thesis. From literally the cradle to the grave, modern liberalism now provides a person with an animating purpose. Children shouldn't merely be taught reading, writing, and arithmetic; they should also learn to treasure Mother Earth and to value "tolerance, inclusion, and diversity." College students learn how the present society needs to be remade from the ground up, how men's "belief systems must be rebuilt" to treat women as equals. Employers must concentrate on creating workplaces that "welcome" alternative lifestyles. Investors must invest only in "socially responsible" companies. Television shows must cast gay individuals in the most positive light.

Literally no area of life is immune to the liberal reach. Christina Hoff Summers's revealing book, *The War Against Boys,* exposes the feminist left's use of millions of dollars of taxpayer money to reeducate and remake young children. In *PC, M.D.,* Dr. Sally Sotel details how medical research dollars, health-care strategies, and even individual treatment decisions are subject to the pervasive influence of political correctness. David Brooks's influential book *BoBos in Paradise* takes a humorous but insightful look at how contemporary politics impacts everything from career choices to oven purchases.

The purpose of this book is not to repeat the arguments or the research of others who have (much more capably than I) painstakingly shown how the left attempts to influence every corner of modern life. Nor is it my intention to argue that the left is the only party engaged in such activity. Virtually every self-respecting evangelical does the same thing. We want people to become Christians, and when they do, we want their Christianity to impact everything about their lives. We want people to raise their children in the "fear and admonition of the Lord." We would prefer that Christians are portrayed positively on television and the rest of the media. We seek Christian businesses to patronize and Christian schools to educate us. Truth be told, some of us even begin to root for a particular sports team when we learn one or more of the prominent players is Christian. (In fact, the St. Louis Rams became one of my favorite NFL teams when I learned that Kurt Warner is not only a great quarterback but also an outspoken evangelical.)

I will not argue why the Christian view is correct and the liberal left is misguided. Nor will I argue that liberals should not see their political/religious views as impacting every aspect of their lives. If individuals deeply believe America is in the grip of a homophobic, racist, patriarchal hegemony, then they are cowardly and timid if they do not act on those beliefs and oppose the powers they perceive as evil. I respect the passion of the left and am sometimes jealous of that passion as I survey the dead eyes and dull faces that too often occupy the pews of America's evangelical churches.

However, what I will argue—and what I hope to prove—is that, in this struggle between two opposing religious ideas, only one is protected by the government. Only one is often actually advanced by the government. And only one is routinely faced with a fight just to have its voice heard. The playing field is not level, and some speech is much more free than others.

In the pages that follow, you will see how the law permits public school liberals to teach views of sexuality and gender roles that are fundamentally inconsistent with evangelical Christianity while denying Christians even the right to opt out of the instruction. You will see how liberal students at secular universities are free to berate Christians and ridicule Christianity while Christian students often struggle just to meet in empty classrooms and sometimes find that their evangelistic words can be punished as hate speech. You will see how the law allows a secular employer to punish religious speech and disregard your religious objections while sometimes preventing you from sharing your faith at work. Because the liberal's speech is "secular" while the Christian's speech is "religious," the government can speak with a liberal voice but cannot speak with a Christian voice. Because the law protects employees against religious harassment but not secular argument, an employer can limit religious speech while subjecting religious employees to truly offensive secular presentations and policies. In other words, the law allows the liberal to indoctrinate while sometimes denying Christians even the opportunity to persuade.

I am not satisfied, however, with merely pointing out the problems with modern, secular government. Too many Christians are content to sit back and complain—to moan about the evils of liberals everywhere and long for the alleged purity of the inaccurately remembered past. This book instead presents a proposed solution to the legal imbalances that plague American life, but this solution will not sit well with some. I will not argue that the government should take our side in the great moral debate. There is simply no chance that a minority as small as evangelical America could ever turn a government into an instrument of theological purity. Nor should we even want to try. The answer to imbalance is not further imbalance. It is not replacing liberal speech codes with government-mandated prayer or other religious observance. The answer is freedom and neutrality. Let's ask the government to take its thumb off the ideological and religious scales.

Simply put, Christians should become leaders in the fight for freedom of expression. All we want is an opportunity to speak—to share our faith. We are not interested in shutting down other points of view, and we are certainly not interested in making the government our instrument of evangelism. The goal of our cultural battles should not be to control a government, or even simply to change individual behavior—it is to change hearts and minds.

In each chapter of this book, I will demonstrate exactly how the law is biased against religious expression—and how this bias pervades and impacts our lives from public school, to college, to the workplace. But these chapters also will end with specific proposals—calls to replace liberal indoctrination not with our own forms of coercion but with true freedom of expression. Let there be a true marketplace of ideas, and may the best Idea—the one Idea that is animated and guided by the Holy Spirit of the living God—win.

3

Grade School Dogma

Fighting Indoctrination in Public Schools

Imagine that you are the parent of a sixteen-year-old boy in a public high school in the northeast. You are nervous—maybe a little frightened. In the last several weeks, your son has started to withdraw from you. Until now he had always seemed happy at home, even during the difficult first two years at high school. Unlike the stereotypical teen, he seemed to enjoy talking to his parents, and he never resented spending time at home. People liked him, and he seemed to like people—but things were changing.

You first noticed the change about six weeks ago, when he brought a new friend home with him. This new guy was nice enough, but you were not sure you liked the way your son behaved when this friend was around. Your son was more sullen, maybe even a little snappy. The two of them spent a lot of time in your son's room, with the door shut, talking in hushed tones.

Your son had always enjoyed playing the guitar, but until now, he had never really hung out with other musicians. But this new friend played the guitar too. So did the other guys who started dropping by. The more time your son spent with them, the less time he spent with you.

Your friends all told you not to worry. It is "just a phase," they would say. Many of them empathized with you.

"My son won't even talk to me anymore."

"My daughter thinks I exist solely to ruin her life."

"My son doesn't even tell me when the school has parent-child events."

You hear your friends, and you try not to worry, but this is your child—not theirs. Your child is not like that. Your child has never been like that. Something else is wrong. Two weeks ago, at dinner, you began to realize what that something else might be.

The table was quiet except for the sound of silverware clinking against plates. You had tried to engage the family in conversation, but no one seemed interested. Your husband was very tired. Work was draining him more than ever, and he felt "talked out" by the time he came home. Your daughter was quiet to begin with—and she was busy eating her favorite meal. Your son broke the silence. "Mom, I'm going to be late coming home from school tomorrow."

"Why?"

"GSA meeting."

"What? What's that?" There was something about the way he mentioned the meeting that bothered you . . .

He paused and picked at his potatoes. "It stands for Gay/Straight Alliance. Look, before you say anything, it's no big deal. It's just a bunch of people who hang out and talk about issues and politics and stuff. Straights and gays. No big deal. Jeff [his new friend] told me it was pretty cool. Thought I'd check it out."

"Well . . ." Your response was a little weak. You regret that now. You let him go without protest, assuming that resistance would only stiffen his determination and widen the gulf between you. Besides, this was an official school club. How bad could it be? You let him go, but you did not drop the issue. Instead you decided to do some research.

Working quickly, you found out the club had a Web site and posted a schedule of activities. Last week was movie night, with a movie name listed. You did not recognize the name, but after just a few minutes on the Internet, you discovered a full synopsis. The movie was described as a "daring portrayal of two young boys' sexual self-discovery" and was rated R for "language, adult situation, and explicit portrayals of gay sex." On the Web site were links to various gay advocacy organizations, some of which linked directly to gay pornography sites and gay dating services. You were stunned.

With your heart pounding, you walked into your son's room. He was not home—visiting Jeff—but he had left his school backpack. It was sitting on the bed, partially unzipped. You could see some papers inside—some school papers, others brightly colored. Without hesitation, you reached in, pulled out a jumble of books, magazines, and notebooks, and began reading.

Most of the materials were innocuous. Science homework. English papers. Spanish workbooks. But some of it was different. From the inside pocket of a notebook labeled "Club Things," you pulled a collection of brochures. The first had a picture of a condom on the cover and was emblazoned with a bold, red title: "Gays Do It Safer!" The next featured a picture of an adult man, his shirt off, smiling provocatively. "Meeting a Good Man: A Queer Dating Guide." You could not even look at the rest. Behind the brochures you found a handwritten note— to your son from Jeff. You did not want to open it, but you did. You had to. With trembling hands and tears in your eyes, you unfolded the paper and began reading . . .

For two days you were literally paralyzed with shock. You had tried to talk to your son, but he was evasive—and outraged at your invasion of his privacy. You called your pastor and the youth pastor, and they offered some comfort but few answers. But behind the shock, you could feel your anger building. A club at your local public school, funded by the school, funded by the state, providing kids with sexually explicit brochures that advocate gay sex and try to facilitate gay dating? A club that schedules as an activity the viewing of sexually explicit gay movies? You are outraged. Someone must be told.

You decide to call the principal. You have met her before, and she seems to be truly kind and fully engaged. Although there are more than fifteen hundred students in your son's school, at a recent basketball game you noticed that she greeted your son by name. She walked out of her way to meet you and congratulate you on raising such a "good son—a real star here at Northside." You knew that she trumpeted an "open door policy" with students, teachers, and parents. She told everyone, "Call me anytime, about anything."

One Friday afternoon you accept her offer and make the call. "Northside's a big school," you assure yourself. "She can't know everything that goes on." The phone rings.

"Northside High." A pleasant voice answers.

"Principal Johnson, please." You notice your voice is shaking. Your hands are sweaty.

"This is Sarah Johnson."

"Ms. Johnson, this is Cathy Young, I'm calling regarding my son, David Young."

"Oh?" You can hear the concern in her voice. "Is there a problem? I'm not aware of anything from my end. David's one of our best."

"Thanks." Her compliment puts you at ease. "I'm not calling because of anything I've heard from a teacher or because of a disciplinary problem. I'm calling . . ." Your voice catches.

"Is everything OK?" The principal's tone moves from concern to alarm.

"Well." You take a deep breath. "David's becoming much more withdrawn. He won't talk to me like he used to, and he's even started defying us and resenting us more than I've ever seen. He's just not himself."

"Really? We haven't noticed that here. At least I haven't heard anyone voice a concern. What's—"

You cut her off. "I'm not calling because he's sullen—a lot of kids are sullen. I'm calling because I think that he's being influenced by some things at your school. Well, not things. A club. He's having problems— I'm having problems—with one of your clubs."

"Which one?"

"The GSA, the Gay/Straight Alliance." You hear the principal sigh, and you plunge ahead. "I don't know if you know this, but I've discovered that they are watching R-rated movies during club meetings, and these movies contain gay sex scenes. I also found out that they've been distributing sexually explicit literature to my son that provides sex and dating advice. Some of these handouts are really very provocative, almost pornographic. Since he's joined the club, I've also learned that he may be in a . . ." Your voice falters. ". . . in a gay relationship. Now I know you probably don't know any of this, and I know that this puts you in a difficult position, but—"

The principal cuts you off. "I know all about this."

You are stunned. "What? You know?"

"Yes. I know what goes on at the GSA." Her voice is no longer warm, and there's no hint of concern. She sounds coolly professional. "In fact, I led the effort to get a GSA chapter at Northside. I want our gay kids to feel like there's a place where they belong. Those brochures are not pornographic. They're informational. Gay teens need to know how they can safely explore their sexuality."

"David is not gay, and I don't send him to school to explore his sexuality. This is really unbelievable. I can't believe a school that I help support is intentionally promoting this kind of behavior. Does the school board know about this?"

"Yes. Yes, they do. They approved the program—at a public meeting."

"I didn't know."

"Ms. Young, do you have any other gay family members? Any way of understanding the gay experience?"

You are too shocked to frame a coherent response. "No, Ms. Johnson, we're Christians, we—"

Once again, she cuts you off. This time, her voice is firm. "Ms. Young, here at Northside, we made a decision that we would not permit homophobia to keep us from serving and nurturing our kids. If you want to come to the school and let me explain the GSA program, I'm more than happy to do that. If you want me to send you GSA literature—literature that can give you a glimpse of the pain and rejection that unsupported gay teens can feel—I'm happy to do that too. But I don't want to talk about fear-based objections to a program that is giving hope to dozens of our kids. Your son's sexuality is his own. He'll have to work that out himself. All GSA does is provide him with a safe place to ask some really tough questions."

You really don't know how to respond. Rage and grief wash over you. "Maybe I'll talk to the school board. I can't believe what I'm hearing."

"Talk to the school board. That's your right. In the meantime I really do have to go. We have a school assembly in ten minutes."

After you hang up, you sit and stare at the phone, tears of rage rolling down your cheeks. "*Your* kids? But I thought he was *my* son—my little boy."

The Sexual Agenda

The scenario recounted above is based in truth. Last year the *Massachusetts News,* a small, family-oriented newspaper, published an exposé that the major media somehow missed. The story detailed exactly how local and state governments use state tax dollars to fund explicit advocacy of graphic homosexual behavior. Unsurprisingly, this story escaped the national media's attention. However, its significance should not escape you.

The story begins in 1999, when a mother from the western suburbs of Boston, Massachusetts, joined with concerned parents to make a "frantic" appeal to the governor's office.[1] Her son had begun attending meetings of the local high school's Gay/Straight Alliance club. The mother soon discovered the club watched at least one R-rated video of two boys "having a love affair." She also discovered some "provocative handouts" in her son's room. Her son became detached, and she suspected he was becoming involved in homosexual relationships.

She complained to the principal, but he would not investigate. No other officials investigated. Instead, "it was suggested that maybe she was homophobic." The governor of Massachusetts, Paul Celucci, would not speak to her, nor would anyone from his office. The parents were able to gain the ear of a public health official, but later the official would not return the mother's calls.

Why would the mother of a possibly gay student appeal to the governor of a state for help with a problem club at a local school? The answer is simple. Each year, the governor budgeted $1.5 million for the "Governor's Commission for Gay and Lesbian Youths." This commission is comprised primarily of gay activists and has used state money to lobby successfully over 180 Massachusetts schools to accept Gay/Straight Alliance clubs. According to the *Massachusetts News,* "The Commission works closely with a national organization, the Gay and

Lesbian and Straight Educational Network (GLSEN), to give the clubs materials, movies, literature and funding for various activities."[2] The purpose of the GSA clubs, according to school officials, is rather modest and seemingly unobjectionable—"to make gay students feel safe."

However, courageous parents and teachers—and the intrepid reporters of the *Massachusetts News*—were not content with these explanations. On 25 March 2000 the Massachusetts Department of Education, the Governor's Commission, and GLSEN cosponsored a statewide conference at Tufts University entitled "Teach Out."[3] The conference was intended to encourage more GSA clubs in the state, and many conference presenters encouraged extending homosexual teaching into the lower grades. "Scores of gay-friendly teachers and administrators attended. They received state 'professional development credits.' Teenagers and children . . . were bussed in from their home districts." Also present were representatives from the *Massachusetts News,* and they took copious notes. A warning: *what you are about to read may shock and offend you.*

One of the workshops at this conference was entitled "What They Didn't Tell You About Queer Sex & Sexuality in Health Class: A Workshop for Youth Only, Ages 14–21." In this class three state officials (two coordinators of the Massachusetts Department of Education's HIV/AIDS Program and one consultant for a similar program from Massachusetts Department of Public Health) talked to "about 20 children" about gay sex.

Throughout the workshop the state officials asked graphic, intrusive questions of the teenage audience—inquiring whether "they knew, as gay people, whether or not they've had sex." Following this discussion, the officials led the children in role-playing exercises. In one exercise, a student played the part of "a young lesbian who's really enraptured with another woman, and it's really coming down to the wire and you're thinking about sex." Her partner in the exercise was a "hip GSA . . . lesbian adviser, who you feel you can talk to." The counseling consisted of "discussions of lesbian sex, oral-vaginal contact, or 'carpet munching' as one student put it."

At this point the presentation became truly appalling. There was a brief pause so that students could write down questions for the state officials teaching the workshop. The first question was, "What's fisting?" The *Massachusetts News* recounts what happened next:

> A student answered this question by informing the class that "fisting" is when you put your "whole hand into the [buttocks] or [vagina]" of another. When a few of the students winced, the Department of Public Health Employee offered, "A little known fact about fisting, you don't make a fist, like this. It's like this," forming his hand into the shape of a tear drop rather than a balled fist. He informed the children that it was much easier . . .
>
> At this point, a child of about 16 asked why someone would want to do that. He stated that if the hand were pulled out quickly, the whole thing didn't sound very appealing to him. [One of the Department of Education officials] was sure to point out that although fisting "often gets a really bad rap," it usually isn't about the pain, "not that we're putting that down." [The official] informed him and the class that "fisting" was "an experience of letting somebody into your body that you want to be that close and intimate with." When a child asked the question, "Why would someone do this?" [the official] provided a comfortable response to the children in order to "put them into an exploratory mode."[4]

And what of the emphasis on student safety? The session ran a full fifty-five minutes before the first mention of safer sex. However, during that discussion it was noted that one could make an "informed decision" not to use a condom.

Another session—taught by the same public officials—was entitled "Putting the 'Sex' Back into Sexual Orientation: Classroom Strategies for Health and Sexuality Educators." This workshop was attended by a "room full of teachers" and featured such comments as "We always feel like we are fighting against people who deny publicly, who say privately, that being queer is not at all about sex. . . . We believe otherwise. We think that sex is central to every single one of us and particularly queer youth." The same officials who gave the scintillating presentation of "fisting" informed the teachers that they would go to their schools and conduct workshops for their students.

Other sessions included a presenter demonstrating how she turned classroom discussions of the holocaust into a section on gay affirmation. This presenter, conducting a workshop called "Struggles & Triumphs of Including Homosexuality in a Middle School Curriculum," also allowed the audience to watch a video she had her students produce. This video was narrated by a seventh-grade girl. This girl told the conferees that ancient Greeks "encouraged homosexuals; in fact, it was considered normal for an adolescent boy to have an older, wiser lover."

These accounts come from only three of the many workshops at this taxpayer-funded conference. Other workshops had titles like: "Getting Gay Issues Included in Elementary School Staff," "Diesel Dykes and Lipstick Lesbians: Defining and Exploring Butch/Femme Identity," and "The Religious Wrong: Dealing Effectively with Opposition in Your Community."

Legal Imbalance

The point of relating that story is not to try to argue that such conferences are common. I do not have empirical evidence that they are. Rather, it provides a shocking example of just how unbalanced the legal playing field is. Because the content of the program was "secular," it was legally acceptable for government officials to use government funds to promote behavior incompatible with evangelical Christianity. In other words, the students and teachers at that seminar cannot practice biblical Christianity and at the same time engage in the behavior (or even hold the views) taught at the workshops. In essence the government is permitted to teach children that their faith—and the faith of their parents—is a "religious wrong."

The conference discussed above was voluntary. No students or teachers were compelled to attend. However, it is important to understand the legal reality that the government's authority is not limited to sponsoring voluntary conferences that refute key elements of the Christian message. The truth is, governments can *compel* children to attend public assemblies that ridicule chastity and blatantly advocate extramarital sex.

When I was a second-year law student, I was part of the Harvard Law School student chapter of the Rutherford Institute, a national religious liberties organization. The president of the student chapter received a call from a local lawyer, asking for help on a new case. He had filed a lawsuit on behalf of a collection of outraged parents and students against a Massachusetts school district and a production company called Hot, Sexy and Safer Productions, Inc.[5] The school district had asked the local judge to dismiss the parents' lawsuit, and the lawyer needed some help with legal research.

The facts of the case were outrageous. At the instigation of some parent members of the Chelmsford, Massachusetts, Parent Teacher

Organization (PTO), the Chelmsford High School had hired Hot, Sexy and Safer to present a "safe sex" program to the students. All students were *required* to attend.

The unsuspecting Christian students filed into the school auditorium, where a local doctor told them that they were about to hear a "special messenger" who "uses probably one of the most effective forms of communication—humor." At that moment, the lead presenter, Suzi Landolphini, bounded on the stage and jauntily informed the students that they were about to have a "group sexual experience with audience participation."

At least one Christian student stood up to leave, but one of the teachers ordered him to stay in his seat. He stayed—and was treated to an hour of graphic sexual instruction. According to the students present, Ms. Landolphini simulated masturbation; described the loose pants worn by one child as "erection wear"; joked about being in "deep sh—" after anal sex; licked an oversized condom with a male student from the audience; asked another male child to show his "orgasm face" with her for a camera; and told another male child that he was not having enough orgasms. She used profane language throughout the presentation and, on at least one occasion, closely inspected a child's body and told him that he had a "nice butt." In short, the students were treated to an hour-long, mandatory program that "advocated and approved oral sex, masturbation, homosexual sexual activity, and condom use during promiscuous premarital sex."

Two fifteen-year-old students and their parents sued. The plaintiffs claimed that the school violated a variety of rights, including the parents' right to direct their child's education and the children's rights to free exercise of religion.

I spent several nights and days working on the case. I researched other cases, read law review articles, and talked to other law students. I even made a point of discussing the case with one of my constitutional law professors. I soon learned that the case was hopeless. The parents' constitutional right to direct their child's education does not encompass a right to opt out of individual school programs—however offensive the parents find the presentation. The child's constitutional right to free exercise of religion does not protect them from government programs that are "neutral" and of "general applicability." Because the program was "secular," did not explicitly target Christianity, and was mandatory for everyone, the Christians had no right to object.

To no one's real surprise, the local federal judge threw the suit out of court. The First Circuit Court of Appeals affirmed the trial court's decision, and the Christians' lawsuit was dead. When I relate the story of Hot, Sexy and Safer Productions to other Christians, many of them express absolute amazement that the case was lost. "Surely," they say, "you can't force students to attend something that offends their beliefs—or their parents' beliefs. Don't we have religious freedom?" Lawyers, on the other hand, tend to be amazed that the parents (and their attorneys) thought they had any chance at all of winning the case. Why this disconnect between public perception and legal reality? Why do Christians always seem incredulous when they begin to understand how limited their rights actually are?

Without question, we live in a rights-obsessed society. We have the right to free speech, the right to counsel, and the right against self-incrimination. We have rights to welfare benefits, to vote, to purchase property, and to work for minimum wages. We have rights to life, to liberty, and to the pursuit of happiness. Virtually every public policy argument is phrased in the language of entitlement—of rights. When I was in college in Nashville, and there was a local move to ban gambling at bingo games, I saw one earnest, elderly voter loudly proclaim that she had "a constitutional right to play bingo." I was shocked when no one laughed. Instead, several fellow demonstrators nodded their heads vigorously.

So in this land of rights, when a parent approaches a school board and asks that his or her child be excused from reading a particular textbook or from attending certain school assemblies or classes, that parent is often stunned when the answer is an emphatic no. What about our rights? While it is true that many local school boards allow parents and children to opt out of certain classes and assemblies, it should be emphasized that they are rarely required to grant that privilege. That decision is often a local political decision created by local political environment. It is rarely a legal imperative mandated by constitutional law.

It is critically important to understand where our rights begin . . . and end. Without this understanding, our outrage lacks a precise target, our activism is wasted on irrelevancies, and we often fight the wrong enemy.

Religious Freedom: A Basic Primer

If you ask the average person what the First Amendment to the United States Constitution says, odds are they will have no idea. Some educated individuals will answer that the amendment guarantees freedom of speech. Others will accurately note that it also protects religious freedom and freedom of the press. A select few may also know that the amendment has something to do with the separation of church and state. Almost no one can quote the amendment, and fewer still (including surprisingly few lawyers) have an even basic understanding of its contemporary meaning.

The complete text of the First Amendment is as follows:

> Congress shall make no law respecting an establishment of religion, or prohibiting the free exercise thereof; or abridging the freedom of speech, or the press; or the

right of the people to peaceably assemble, and to petition the Government for a redress of grievances.

The careful reader will note that there are two distinct ways the government is restricted with respect to religion. The "establishment
clause" of the amendment states that the government cannot establish
a religion. The "free exercise clause" prohibits the government from
unduly restricting the "exercise" or practice of religion.

When a lawsuit is brought against a public school that begins graduation ceremonies with a word of prayer, the plaintiff usually alleges an
establishment clause violation. In other words, by having a government
official (schoolteacher or principal) pray to begin an official meeting of
a government organization (the public school), the school "establishes"
the particular religion of the one who prays. On the other hand, when
a lawsuit is brought against a public school because they are preventing
a Christian club from meeting on campus, the plaintiff usually alleges
a free exercise clause violation. By preventing the Christians from meeting together for prayer, worship, and teaching, the school prohibits the
"free exercise" of the students' religion.

Millions of pages have been written and tens of millions of words
spoken about the establishment clause and the free exercise clause.
From childhood, I heard about "America's Christian heritage." I learned
that many (but not all) of our founding fathers were deeply spiritual
Christians who believed that the American experiment was doomed
unless its people remained faithful to God. I also learned that the establishment clause was not written to strip prayer from the public schools
but to protect the official state churches of the original thirteen colonies
from a possible federal church. Many of the first states were officially
affiliated with different Christian denominations, and those state officials were afraid that the federal government would take away their
autonomy. The establishment clause protected those state churches.

I learned that as recently as forty years ago, many schools began their days with Scripture readings and heartfelt prayers. Finally, I learned that our schools began to decline "the minute" we took prayer out of schools.

In college, I became truly fascinated by this history. I read virtually everything I could get my hands on. When I was admitted to Harvard, I redoubled my studies. I knew that I was going into a lion's den of secularism, and I not only wanted to survive—I wanted to butcher the lions with my knowledge, reasoning, and arguments. I thought my classmates would be impressed by the lost history of our forefathers.

I was so naive. Not only were my secular friends not persuaded by historical arguments, the knowledge that George Washington or Alexander Hamilton thought that Christianity was critical to our national life made some of my classmates more eager to believe the opposite. They did not want to learn from these "slave-owning, dead white males"; they actively wanted to distance themselves—and this country—from their "terrible legacy." The history of the First Amendment was irrelevant. They wanted to know what the amendment meant now.

I made a terrible mistake. I assumed that facts important to me would also be important to them. I assumed we spoke the same language. I did not realize how thoroughly my evangelical Christian worldview colored how I processed information and formed ideas. I read the law like I read the Bible. As I explained in the previous chapter, when I came across a statute or a regulation, I read the words and tried to apply the words as I understood them. If I could not understand the words, I would try to learn about the intent of the writers. What did they want to accomplish with this law? What was the wrong they were trying to remedy? How can we accomplish what they were attempting to accomplish?

My fellow students' methods were completely different. Many of them had made up their minds about a statute's meaning. It meant whatever it needed to mean to further their particular agenda. The only interesting discussion was how to shape the actual words to fit the desired meaning. Others were primarily interested in the racial, religious, and sexual identity of the authors. If the authors were corrupt to them in any one of innumerable ways (slave owners, classist, racist, homophobic, patriarchal), then the text itself was suspect and worthy of scorn. History was only important if it discredited "unjust" law.

My classmates' philosophies were diverse, but they generally shared an interest in the present and the future. My historical discoveries were irrelevant. They wanted to know what the establishment clause meant now and what it would mean ten years from now. They wanted to know how they could shape society by altering the meaning of the clause and how they could right past wrongs by disregarding "original intent."

And they had a point. The Constitution is not holy Scripture. It was not written by God. It is therefore legitimate to argue that its meaning is not fixed in eternity. Why did I always have to argue from the past? Slowly, I began to realize that I needed to understand what the First Amendment means today and what it will potentially look like in the future. I needed to build a new legal philosophy—a new method of discourse. While my old methods were appropriate for roundtable discussions with fellow Christians, they were completely inadequate to address the secular decision makers who hold the reins of power.

Establishing a Religion?

On 15 June 1994 the United States Court of Appeals for the Ninth Circuit made a decision that generated almost no media publicity.[6] The court's opinion used conventional reasoning to dispose of a rather routine challenge to educational practices. The elite media—which usually cannot seem to pass up an opportunity to embarrass the "religious right"—issued a collective yawn. When extremist groups assert extreme claims, it is hardly national news when those claims are denied.

In this case, the extremist group was the American Family Association, and their extremist clients were Douglas and Katherine Brown, parents of two public school students, and members of the Assembly of God denomination. The Browns objected to their local school district's decision to teach literature from the "Impressions" textbook series. Impressions is a widely used series of fifty-nine books that contains several thousand literary selections and suggested classroom activities. Impressions takes a "whole language" approach to reading instruction. Literary selections are followed by suggested classroom activities, such as having children role-play the selections, compose poetry, or discuss the selections' characters and themes.

The vast majority of the literary selections are uncontroversial. In fact, the series as a whole is rather conventional. In their review of the material, however, the Browns noted some disturbing reading and activities buried within the books. The Browns challenged thirty-two selections—virtually all of which dealt specifically with the religion of Wicca or witchcraft. Many of the challenged sections asked students to pretend that they were witches and sorcerers and actually cast spells. Other sections asked children to compose poetic chants.

The Browns' objection was simple—and sensible. Because practitioners of Wicca are known as sorcerers or witches, and because spell-casting and charms are sacred rituals of this religion, isn't the school "establishing" the Wiccan religion when it requires students to engage in quintessentially Wiccan activities?

Thus far, the case seems straightforward. Surely, you think, the Browns will win. Imagine if a public school teacher required students to role-play as priests or pastors and compose hymns to Jesus. Undoubtedly the teacher would be disciplined, the practice abandoned, and, quite possibly, money damages paid to offended students. How could Wicca be favored over Christianity? or Judaism? or Islam?

The law is not so simple. Although the Browns were able to prove that the Impressions exercises mimicked Wiccan religious practice, it turns out that this similarity may have been quite accidental. The author-editors of Impressions "were unfamiliar with the religion of witchcraft," and "neither the author-editors nor the publisher had any aim of promoting or endorsing any religious practices, including witch-craft." In the court's view the challenged sections involved no more than "merely reading, discussing, or contemplating witches, their behavior, or witchcraft."

All the evidence, taken together, demonstrated that the Browns were challenging ostensibly religious exercises assigned without religious intent. In other words, the author-editors wanted the children to learn about witches, not necessarily become witches themselves. Requiring children to engage in religious rituals was a component of the particular teaching method, not part of a plan of proselytization.

Typically, when a court attempts to determine whether a person or corporation or government's actions are illegal, they compare the actions to a specific legal standard, or "test." In this case, the appropriate establishment clause test was well-known. Since the 1971 case of *Lemon v. Kurtzman,* the Supreme Court of the United States has required that all government programs (1) have a "secular purpose"; (2) have a "primary effect" that neither advances nor inhibits religion; and (3) not foster "excessive state entanglement with religion."[7]

Although the *Lemon* Test has been criticized—even by members of the Supreme Court—it is still the law of the land. If a governmental organization is charged with violating the establishment clause of the Constitution, then, in almost every case, the *Lemon* Test is applied.

By carefully reading the *Lemon* Test and applying it to various church-state controversies, you can begin to understand why school prayer is always banned, why the Ten Commandments have been taken from schoolhouse walls, and why cities almost never sponsor Christmas nativity scenes. How can school prayer have a "secular purpose"? Is not prayer, by definition, an appeal to the supernatural—the spiritual? The Ten Commandments are considered by many to be the founding moral document of Judaism and a bulwark of the Christian worldview. How can a government post them in classrooms without advancing those two religions? If a government places a nativity scene alone in a public park, doesn't that indicate that the government itself is honoring Christianity? How does that demonstrate a "secular purpose"? How can that have any effect but the advancement of Christianity?

The *Lemon* Test presented the Browns with an interesting challenge. Because there was no evidence that the author-editors of Impressions (or anyone else) sought to advance witchcraft, the Browns had to concede the first prong—that the school board had a "secular purpose" when it adopted the schoolbooks. The Browns also had to concede the third prong. There was no real argument that the books fostered "excessive entanglement" with the Wiccan religion. Consequently, the Browns' entire establishment clause case rested on the second prong— that mandatory spell-casting, poetic chanting, and witch role-playing had the "primary effect" of advancing witchcraft.

Again, this was a sensible argument. To win on this prong, all the Browns had to prove was that the government practice (enforced spell-casting) was "sufficiently likely to be perceived by adherents of the controlling denominations as an endorsement, and by the nonadherents as a disapproval, of their individual religious choices." The relevant inquiry was "whether the government's action actually conveys a message of endorsement of religion in general or of a particular religion."

Here, the Browns seemed sure to win. The government was endorsing a particular religious practice so strongly they were actually requiring children to participate in it.

But the Browns lost. The court held that the Woodland Joint Unified School District was not establishing the Wiccan religion. Why not? Basically, the case turned on perceptions. If the government is prohibited from "conveying a message of endorsement," who decides when the message is conveyed? The Browns said that a message of endorsement was conveyed when the child in the classroom believed that the government was endorsing the religious practice. The court disagreed. A message of endorsement is conveyed only when the "reasonable observer" believes it is conveyed. This observer must be "informed as well as reasonable." And who, really, is this informed, reasonable observer? It is the court.

In the informed, reasonable view of the court, an "objective" person would realize that Impressions' arguably Wiccan sections were but a "minute" fraction of the total body of work. This same objective person would also realize that, although the textbooks contained ideas consistent with Wicca, "mere consistency with religious tenets" is insufficient to constitute "religious endorsement." The "objective" observer would also realize the spell-casting exercises "are not formal religious rituals." At best, the court said, the Browns could prove only that children would perceive them as such. Consequently, the Browns could not prove (objectively) that the government was endorsing any religious practice, and their case was dismissed.

Think back a moment to the title of a previous section: "Legal Imbalance." For the evangelical Christian, the establishment clause truly does create a wall of separation between church and state. Because our purposes are never "secular," we cannot even cross the first hurdle of the *Lemon* Test. There is simply no way we can explicitly, "officially" teach Christ to public school children.

For the liberal, however, the establishment clause is meaningless. Because their purposes are almost always explicitly "secular," and because the "objective" view of the courts insulates leftist teachings (and even occasionally fringe religious practices) from constitutional challenge, there is no legal barrier to explicitly, "officially" teaching doctrines that stand directly against Christ. Because the scope of modern liberalism is so vast—touching on virtually every area of public and private life, from private sexual behavior to marital power dynamics to racial understanding to economic justice, and so on—the local public school can launch a comprehensive assault on virtually everything a Christian student believes, and there is nothing the courts will do to stop them.

Both sides hold beliefs with religious intensity. Only one can use the government to get out its message. Those two sentences are a virtually complete explanation for the contemporary Christian exodus from public schools.

Shards of Freedom

As I discussed before, the religion clauses of the First Amendment fulfill a critical double purpose. First, the establishment clause of the First Amendment "forestalls compulsion by law of the acceptance of any creed or the practice of any form of worship." In other words, freedom of conscience and the freedom to choose and belong to a religion or religious organization cannot be restricted by law. Second, the free exercise clause protects the freedom to practice your chosen form of religion. "Thus the Amendment embraces two concepts—freedom to believe and freedom to act."[8]

However, the freedom to act is not unlimited. The government, which includes public schools, may restrict religious freedom under certain circumstances.

The precise extent of the government's ability to regulate religious practice is the subject of much misunderstanding. Recent changes in the law have led many public school officials to believe they have virtually unlimited authority to regulate the religious practices of students, faculty, and religious organizations. This view, however, is terribly mistaken. In fact, in recent years, the trend has been quite the opposite: religious individuals and organizations are gaining *increasing* levels of freedom.

Much of the confusion surrounding religious freedom claims concerns the proper "test" for government action. In 1963, the Supreme Court decided the case of *Sherbert v. Verner.*[9] In *Sherbert,* a woman challenged the state's decision to deny her unemployment compensation simply because she refused to accept employment on Saturday, the Sabbath Day of her faith. The Supreme Court held that the state violated the free exercise clause of the First Amendment when it conditioned the receipt of a government benefit (unemployment compensation) on a change in religious practice (Sabbath rest).

This decision, by itself, was unremarkable. What set *Sherbert* apart, however, was the legal standard it introduced. Justice Brennan, writing for the Court, stated that if a government action imposes a significant burden on religious practice, that action can be justified only (1) if it advances a "compelling state interest" and (2) if "no alternative forms of regulation" would suffice. Unless both prongs of the test could be satisfied, the government action would be invalid.

The *Sherbert* standard represented a significant advance in free exercise jurisprudence and provided significant protection for religious liberties. Why? Because it was often difficult—though not impossible—for the government to prove its religion-restrictive regulations were justified by "compelling" interests. Courts are justifiably reluctant to believe that a government is compelled to limit individual freedoms.

In 1990, however, the standard changed. In *Employment Division v. Smith,*[10] the Supreme Court decided the case of two individuals punished for the religious use of peyote, a hallucinogenic drug. Peyote is ingested for sacramental purposes during some ceremonies of the Native American Church. The Supreme Court upheld the State of Oregon's decision to deny unemployment benefits to the individuals, and, in so doing, changed more than two decades of precedent.

No longer would the government be required to demonstrate that its regulations furthered a "compelling state interest" and that no alternative forms of regulation would suffice. Instead, the government need only demonstrate that religious practice was burdened by a "valid and neutral law of general applicability." In other words, so long as the government was not specifically targeting religious practice, the free exercise clause, by itself, would not protect individuals from the state.

In the controversy that followed this decision, many governmental bodies ignored critical elements of the Supreme Court's ruling. First, the Court clearly stated that state action toward religious organizations must be *neutral.* In other words, the government—although freed from the "compelling state interest" standard—could not enact laws designed primarily (or even partially) to suppress the practice of religion.

Second, while free exercise claims by themselves were weakened by *Smith,* it remained possible for religious individuals and groups to "couple" or "bundle" their free exercise rights with other constitutional rights. In other words, if a religious individual is confronted with a government policy that burdens its religious practice, then he often may claim that not only his free exercise rights have been violated but also his rights to free speech and free association.

These elements are critical. Public school officials, often eager to impose their secular orthodoxy on campus, sometimes seem to view the *Smith* decision as granting them a free hand to regulate religious practice on campus. Nothing could be further from the truth. Campus policies that inhibit religious practices without also inhibiting rights of free speech and association are rare indeed.

In sum, for a public school or other governmental body legally to regulate religious practice on campus, the regulation in question must (1) be neutral *and* (2) not inhibit the exercise of other related constitutional freedoms. If a public school engages in viewpoint discrimination by limiting specific religious practice, or by denying a benefit to a religious group or individual that it offers to other religious groups or to secular organizations, then its actions almost certainly will be illegal.

What Does It Mean to Be "Religious"?

Religious freedom rights are not limited to adherents of mainstream religious groups, or to fundamentalist Christians, or to Orthodox Jews. Religious freedom rights are not the exclusive province even of those who define themselves as particularly "religious." It is an unfortunate (and common) misperception that only those individuals who attend church or synagogue regularly care about or are impacted by religious freedom issues. This misperception often leads to individual indifference toward religious liberty issues and often harmful ignorance when your own rights are trampled.

The right to free exercise of religion is not limited by conventional or orthodox understandings of what religion is or what religious practice consists of. The religion clauses of the First Amendment are almost better understood as guardians of your freedom of conscience—of your own ideas of the Ultimate, or God, in your life.

Although the Supreme Court never has precisely defined religion, it is clear that religious freedom protections are given breathtakingly broad scope.

First, it is clear that you do not have to define yourself as specifically "religious" to receive constitutional protections. In *Welsh v. United States*,[11] the Supreme Court reviewed the case of an individual who sought conscientious objector status under a statute that exempts from military service individuals who by reason of "religious training and belief" are conscientiously opposed to war in any form. This individual, however, stated that he could not affirm or deny belief in a "Supreme Being" and struck the words "my religious training" from the form that requested the exemption. Welsh was subsequently convicted for refusing to accept induction into the armed services. Reversing that conviction, the Supreme Court found that Welsh's beliefs—specifically, that the taking of any life was morally wrong—were more than "a merely personal honor code" and were held with "the strength of more traditional religious convictions." Consequently, he was entitled to receive the "religious" exemption to military service.

Second, it is also clear that if you do define yourself as religious, you do not have to belong to a theistic religion to receive the protection of the religion clauses of the Constitution. The Supreme Court specifically rejected any limitation of "religion" to theistic religions in *Torcaso v. Watkins,*[12] a case invalidating a Maryland constitutional provision requiring appointees to public office to declare a belief in the existence of God. In extending protection to the secular humanist who was challenging the Maryland law, Justice Black specifically listed a number of prominent, nontheistic religions, citing "Buddhism, Taoism, Ethical Culture, Secular Humanism and others."

Third, religious protections are not limited to members of "an organized religious organization." In *Frazee v. Illinois Department of Employment Security,*[13] the Supreme Court allowed a Christian who was not a member of an established religion or sect to receive unemployment benefits, despite his refusal to work on Sundays. Justice White, writing for a unanimous court, explained that the protection of the free exercise clause was not limited to those "responding to the commands of a particular religious organization."

Fourth, if you belong to a religious organization, you can assert religious freedom claims even if your views differ from those of your church or from other members of your religion. In *Thomas v. Review Board of Indiana Employment Security Division*,[14] the Supreme Court reversed Indiana's decision to deny unemployment benefits to a Jehovah's Witness who terminated his job because his religious beliefs forbade participation in the production of armaments. Indiana courts had apparently found that Thomas's views regarding the production of tank turrets apparently differed from those of other Jehovah's Witnesses. Consequently, because Thomas's views were not the views of his "religion," his religious claims were less credible. The Supreme Court emphatically disagreed, holding " . . . it is not within the judicial function and judicial competence to inquire whether the petitioner or his fellow worker more correctly perceived the commands of their common faith. Courts are not arbiters of scriptural interpretation."

Clearly then, the free exercise clause does not just protect mainstream members of "established" churches. It protects the rights of all individuals who hold sincere and meaningful beliefs about ultimate issues in life. State actions that strike at those beliefs, that offend your conscience, may very well implicate the First Amendment. Do not limit your liberty—or shrink back in the face of repression—simply because your conscience places you outside the mainstream of American life, or because your "church" is small, or because no one else shares your views. It is for you that these liberties exist.

The School Prayer Trap

I am just barely old enough to remember school prayer. Although much of my school life was lived after the Supreme Court outlawed official school prayer and after the Court ordered that the Ten Commandments be removed from school walls, it often takes years for public behavior to change. In Scott County, Kentucky—far from the eye of the courts—things changed very slowly.

In fact, even up to my last years of high school, I distinctly remember seeing the Ten Commandments on the wall of every single one of my classrooms. My fifth-grade teacher began each class day with a prayer and a Bible reading. I remember prayers over public address systems, prayers at graduation, and—most definitely—prayers before sporting events.

You might think I have fond memories of those days, the last moments of America's golden age of public Christianity. You might think I felt warmth and affirmation from my fifth-grade teacher's gentle Bible readings. You also might think I was thankful to attend a school that consecrated each day, each significant sporting event, and each graduation with prayer.

You would be wrong. I remember my class Bible readings very well. I remember students squirming through reading time, snickering when the teacher mispronounced a biblical name. I remember the childish, sacrilegious jokes: "I'm hungry. Let's eat communion." I cannot recall a single student who ever expressed anything but frustration that we had to sit and listen to the Bible.

And what about school prayer? When we argue for school prayer, do we actually remember what it was like? These prayers, though often sincere, were more often formulaic and constituted religious compromises—efforts to be prayerful while offending as few people as possible. "Dear God, thanks for the many blessings. Please protect us and watch out for us as we [study, play this game, go forth into the world]. Amen." Other prayers may have been more ornate, but they were all, essentially, the same—a general prayer of thanks, a general prayer of protection/blessing, a general closing.

Even in my small, conservative hometown, there were dozens of churches and dozens of different religious traditions. Students, teachers, and invited clergy seemed happy to pray but eager not to offend. Consequently, any prayer was generic, as "inclusive" as it could possibly be. Public school prayer is not the saints of God, on their knees, doing battle in the heavenlies against an enemy who seeks to devour the souls of children. It is instead a ritual, a tradition, often a collection of platitudes mouthed in monotone by speakers who may or may not believe even a fraction of what they say.

More distressing than the prayers were my classmates' reactions to them. The student reaction to public prayer ran a gamut from indifference to hostility. Most dutifully bowed their heads, but some looked around, spoke to their friends, or worse, mocked the prayer and the student/teacher/preacher who was praying. I never volunteered to pray. I did not like the prayer I was expected to deliver and liked even less the reaction it was sure to generate. We were praying to the God of the universe, the almighty Creator, and my precious Savior—and no one cared.

I lived in the midst of school prayer, the Ten Commandments, and abundant public religiosity, yet at times I felt like a member of a tiny, embattled minority. As a freshman, I did not meet a single person who shared my beliefs. By my junior year I had achieved the reputation of "do-gooder" and "geek." I was one of the few who did not drink, have premarital sex, or experiment with drugs. My high school had one of the higher teen pregnancy rates in the area, and we also had a race problem that almost tore the school apart.

My beautiful high school experience reached its peak at the tail end of my senior year. I was sitting in my world civilization class when I heard yelling, banging, then the unmistakable shriek "Fight! Fight!" One of my friends jumped up and opened the door on a small riot. No less than twenty kids were in the middle of an all-out brawl. Within seconds, approximately forty guys—half of them white and the other half black—were beating each other as hard as they could. Male teachers who waded into the fray were being knocked down or thrown into lockers. Terrified, I shrank back into class.

The fight stopped when more male teachers arrived—and when someone yelled, "The cops are coming! The cops are coming!" Some students ran off; others limped off. Blood was on the floor, and the air was thick with hate.

Subsequent police investigations revealed that the fight started when a white student was thrown out of class for using a vile racial epithet. Rather than go to the principal's office as he was ordered, he ran through the halls yelling more racial insults. Black and white students poured out of their classes, and the battle was joined.

For several days after the riot, armed guards patrolled the halls of the school. I'll never forget looking up from my lunch and seeing a shotgun-toting sheriff's deputy patrolling our cafeteria. The year ended peacefully—not because there was any healing or reconciliation, but because the offenders had been punished, and everyone feared the law.

In May 1987 I walked the graduation line with slightly more than two hundred other seniors. My freshman class numbered almost four hundred, but dozens of my classmates had dropped out of school. Several friends were not in the graduation line because they were home taking care of their new babies. Several who were present were either drunk or stoned. Others spent most of graduation morning planning how they were going to get "drunk, stoned, or laid" later that night. Still others talked about how much they hated someone near them—and that they hoped they did not have to "beat them down" in front of everyone.

Oh yes, I almost forgot. Somebody prayed at graduation.

Ten years later—ten years after I had vowed never to return to Scott County High School—I came back. One of the students in our local church youth group—the same youth group I discussed in chapter 1—asked me to speak at a club meeting. The name of the club was SWAT, Students With a Testimony. I was intrigued and asked a few questions about the club. The student told me the entire history.

"Two years ago, my brother was reading about school prayer—wondering why we didn't have it anymore and wondering if he could pray if he was named valedictorian. Anyway, he came across a pamphlet written by some Christian legal group, and he read that he had the right to start a Christian club on campus if the school let other clubs meet. So he started it."

"How big is it?" I knew how big SWAT would have been when I was in school. I would have been able to count the members on the fingers of both hands.

"I don't know. We fill up the new auditorium classroom. I think we're the biggest club in school."

"I'll do it." The biggest club at school? I had to see for myself. I was already amazed by the size and activity of my church's youth group and was looking forward to seeing all those kids in their "native habitat." Plus, I was curious as to who else would come. A dozen more? Two dozen?

I arrived at ten minutes before 10:00 A.M. on Friday. The school gave all the clubs an hour on Fridays for meetings. My youth group friend was there to meet me. He gave me some advice. "Don't be afraid really to challenge us. Not everyone who comes is real serious about their faith. Most of them are, but we really try to challenge people at these meetings."

I nodded my agreement as the bell rang and the kids came in. The first wave of students were "my" Trinity kids—the kids I knew from church. They brought in some of their friends and began making introductions.

"Hey, David, this is Katrina. She doesn't really come to SWAT, but I told her she *had* to hear you."

"Dave, what's up, man? This is my boy, Brian. He's president of FCA."

"Hey! This is Jill. She's treasurer of SWAT."

As I shook hands and tried to remember names, I noticed the classroom was filling. I estimated the room seated approximately two hundred, and by five minutes after ten, all the seats were taken. By 10:10, there were people lining the walls. I was astounded.

I don't recall exactly what I said that morning, but I do remember challenging them to give everything for Christ. I spoke the Word, and I prayed with intensity and emotion. I had to speak loudly because the public address system was malfunctioning, but no one used my unamplified voice as an excuse to tune out or to begin their own conversations. Every eye was glued to me. Every ear seemed to be listening. When I finished, they hit me with a wave of enthusiastic applause.

Driving away, back to the office, I was profoundly moved. I saw hunger in people's eyes—hunger for the gospel. "Was that Scott County?" "Was that a public school—my old public school?"

Something had changed. Something fundamental.

Revolution—from the Grass Roots

By 1991 America's evangelicals were faced with a bleak landscape. Formal school prayer had been prohibited, the Ten Commandments had been snatched from school walls, and graduation prayer was on shaky ground. To make matters worse, the *Smith* decision (see p. 65) seemed to have dealt a mortal blow to the free exercise clause. Public schools were being cleansed of the last vestiges of Christianity, and the religious rights of individual public school students were at their lowest ebb. Put another way, barring a miracle, Christianity faced extinction in America's public schools.

In the ten years since that dark time, the situation has changed . . . dramatically. Although the establishment clause bars public religious activity, and the free exercise clause is still greatly weakened, many of our public schools are experiencing what can only be described as a religious revival. Events like "See You at the Pole" have morphed from an individual youth group activity into a national movement. Clubs like

Scott County, Kentucky's SWAT dot the public school landscape. Tens of thousands of young people crowd into youth rallies and Christian concerts. In the aftermath of the Columbine massacre, more than seventy thousand teens attended revival services at the Pontiac Silverdome in Detroit. In fact, statistical evidence is beginning to confirm that, for the first time in memory, more teens are attending Bible clubs than taking hard drugs.[15]

What happened? God moved—mightily. Finally, tens of thousands of Christian students and Christian parents were faced with a reality that existed long before it was realized—God was not coming through the government. Instead, the government was opposing God. Congressional votes and political activism were not going to change that fact. Mere support for school prayer was not going to save souls.

For the world to change, individual Christians realized that they had to start at home—in their own school and in their own hearts. Evangelical outcasts banded together, true rebels against a disapproving society. They formed informal clubs and then petitioned schools to grant them the same access and recognition and opportunities that the schools gave the Young Democrats or the Young Republicans. All they needed was a room and a time.

Schools resisted. The Supreme Court's unmitigated hostility to public religion had led many school officials to believe erroneously that the mere expression of Christian thought on a public school campus was illegal. Case databases contain reference after reference to attempts to confiscate student Bibles or to prevent Christian students from delivering book reports or public speeches about Jesus. Marx was acceptable. Nietzsche was acceptable. Jesus was not.

But when schools resisted, God raised up a small but potent army of lawyers, pastors, and legislators who presented a simple, compelling argument: treat us the same. Even if the *Smith* decision had stripped religion of its *special* constitutional status, we still had a right to at least *equal* treatment. If the school was going to open its doors to meetings of civic groups, political groups, and artistic societies, how could it close its doors to Christians—and Christians only? Even the watered-down free exercise clause barred that kind of active discrimination.

In dozens of cases prosecuted by courageous Christian lawyers such as Jay Sekulow of the American Center for Law and Justice, John Whitehead of the Rutherford Institute, and Michael McConnell of the University of Utah, Christians appealed for equality. Nothing more; nothing less. Just give us the same chance you give everyone else. Give us a place in the marketplace of ideas. If our message has no force or relevance in today's world, we cannot be a cause for concern. If, on the other hand, the cross still resonates, no one can say they were forced to bow their knee.

The argument worked. In the seminal case of *Lamb's Chapel v. Moriches Free School District*,[16] the Supreme Court held that a school system that allowed its rooms to be used after-hours for discussion of family and civic issues could not prohibit the use of rooms for discussions of those same issues from a religious perspective. Various legislative enactments, like the Equal Access Act, required government facilities that opened their doors to the community to give equal access to Christians. Most recently, the Supreme Court decisively held that even elementary schools—places long "protected" from "religious influence"—had to allow Christians to use school facilities if it opened the facilities to other groups.

Not only did the argument work, it united Christians, and it opened lines of communication with non-Christians. Baptists worked with Catholics, and atheists worked with Pentecostals—all to ensure that every voice had a chance to be heard.

Instead of relying on government, Christians turned to God. Legal victories like *Lamb's Chapel* only gave us empty classrooms. To fill the empty classrooms, individual Christians had to summon the courage to approach their friends and their friends' friends and invite them to come to meetings—come and get to know Christ.

Christian students, their parents, and youth leaders simply lived the Great Commission. They went out into the public schools and—from their empty classrooms and hallway prayer meetings—preached Christ and Him crucified. The Great Commission does not ask us to go to the king and tell him to make us all pray. The Great Commission is not discharged when we vote for leaders who pray. *We* must go, and *we* must speak.

The Trinity Assembly of God youth group, Scott County's chapter of SWAT, and thousands of similar organizations scattered across the country are the product of basic freedom, Christian courage, and the awesome power of the Holy Spirit. Faithful Christians knew that if only they were given a chance to speak, their world would change. Of all the conflicting voices that students hear as they march from kindergarten to young adulthood, only one is the voice of the Holy Spirit. So long as that voice is heard, lives will change.

The Solution—Freedom and Equality

Today we stand at an interesting impasse. From the top (the educational establishment, the local school boards, and even local teachers), the new religion of liberalism is drummed into the minds of the youth. The state is free to use all of its considerable resources, powers of persuasion, and instruments of coercion to indoctrinate its children into the new American civic religion. But from the bottom, from the children themselves, comes an opposing force. Exercising the basic freedoms that still remain, first thousands, then tens of thousands, now hundreds of thousands turned their back on the state's message and turned their hearts to Jesus.

Where do we—parents, businessmen, doctors, lawyers, plumbers, legislators, and homemakers—fit into this struggle of public indoctrination versus grassroots "rebellion"? One answer is easy. We support our Christian children. We give them our time, we give them our testimonies, we give them our talents, and we even give them our money. If a school board disobeys the law and shuts down a Christian club or denies access to its facilities, we make our voice heard. We attend school board meetings, we write our legislators, and, if absolutely necessary, we take legal action.

Make no mistake; if you pledge to support your community's children, if you work to see that every school at every level has a Christian club, you will face opposition. In chapter 1, I detailed how a local zoning board acted to shut down youth worship. The zoning board's action was outrageous and illegal, but it took courageous church leadership to fight the power of local government. Leaders of America's new liberal religion will fight to silence you, but you must remain vigilant. If your children are silenced, you must speak.

But that is only half the story. What can we do about public indoctrination? This is the battle that we are losing—with terrible consequences. Sadly, some children are exposed only to the message of false tolerance and religious bigotry. They do not have Christian friends, or perhaps their school does not have a Christian club. What aid can we give those students?

Christian America's favorite answer seems to be to fight one form of indoctrination with another, weaker form. On 26 December 2000 the *Washington Times* reported on a new bill that a Virginia lawmaker intended to submit to the Virginia General Assembly. This lawmaker, Richard H. Black, had surveyed local public schools and was concerned: "The counterculture revolution of the '70s took the war into the classroom. Before that time, public schools were a model of decorum, and then we began this thing we've seen play out at Columbine."[17]

Mr. Black hoped that his bill would provide at least part of the answer to the spiritual/cultural crisis in America's schools. His solution was a bill that required students to address teachers as *Ma'am* or *Sir,* and *Mr.* and *Miss* or *Mrs.* At the same time, a fellow legislator planned to introduce a bill requiring all students to recite the Pledge of Allegiance.

In my educational and legal career, I've attended numerous meetings of conservatives and Christian conservatives. I've attended Federalist Society events and Christian Coalition meetings. I joined the College Republicans, and I briefly campaigned for George Bush Sr. in 1988. I attended a Rutherford Institute convention and attended speeches by leaders of the American Center for Law and Justice. I can honestly say that each of these groups, and each of the prominent speakers at the various conventions and meetings, endorsed formal school prayer, required recitations of the pledge of allegiance, or both. For years, I nodded vigorously when a speaker thundered that America was founded as a "Christian nation," and how outrageous it was that "students can be taught about condoms by public officials but they can't be allowed to hear a public official pray."

When the issue is framed like that, it is hard not to be outraged. How is it just that a Massachusetts public school can subject students to a "Hot, Sexy, and Safer" presentation but cannot legally open a graduation service with a brief, nondenominational prayer? Obviously, there is no justice in that situation. However, school prayer is *not* the answer.

I will say that again. School prayer is *not* the answer. Not only is it not *the* answer; it is not even a partial answer to the spiritual crisis in public schools. Before I explain why, I want to present some facts (legal and otherwise) that I believe no one can credibly dispute:

- Evangelical Christians[18] constitute a small minority of the public school students in this country, and evangelical

Christians in general constitute a small minority of the total
population.

- Even evangelicals find it difficult to agree on many important
theological issues, including the proper way to pray.
- If the state permits Christian prayers, it must permit prayers
from other religious traditions.
- Many of these other religious traditions are not only incompatible with faith in Christ; they are hostile to Christianity.

If we recognize these truths and think about public school prayer
logically and thoroughly, then we should recognize that the school
prayer movement is self-defeating and possibly dangerous. Even if
evangelicals are a majority (or powerful plurality) in your school district, they are a minority in the vast majority of school districts in
America. School prayers will reflect the religious composition of their
communities. In general, they will be a series of watered-down, uncontroversial, nondenominational proverbs and petitions. Rarely will a
public prayer ask that the "blood of Jesus" cover a student body. Rarely
will a public prayer specifically call for salvation of the lost. At worst,
Christian students in some school districts will be forced to bow their
heads during Muslim prayers or Wiccan incantations. Is that what we
really want?

You may not believe me when I say that school prayer can open the
door to religious influences like Wicca or Islam. I submit that if you
disbelieve me, then you have not traveled much outside of your own
district or experienced education in other states. If school prayer were
reinstituted, school districts across the country would simply transfer
their "tolerance" or "diversity" agenda into the prayers themselves.
While students in Brentwood, Tennessee, would hear Christian prayers
almost exclusively, it is easy to imagine students in Ithaca, New York;
Burlington, Vermont; or Berkeley, California, hearing prayers to God

on Monday, to Allah on Tuesday, the "goddess" on Wednesday, and Buddha on Thursday—with Friday set aside for meditation.

Further, because we will have voluntarily and intentionally ripped the heart out of modern establishment clause jurisprudence, we will have no credible argument that productions like "Hot, Sexy and Safer" are improper in public schools. If we can make people listen to our prayers, how can we argue—in a free society—that people of different beliefs cannot make us watch graphic "safe sex" productions? Instead of demanding that indoctrination stop, we are asking that our indoctrination be added to the mix. That is not a rational thing for an embattled minority to request.

More controversially, what do we really hope to accomplish with school prayer? Are we really expecting to see souls saved? Were our public schools hotbeds of Christianity in the sixties and seventies when public school prayer (or at least prominent displays of the Ten Commandments) were the norm? In fact, the generation that created the liberal counterculture was a generation raised on public religiosity.

I have often heard it said that America's schools began their downward spiral when prayer was removed. Certainly, there is a correlation between prayerless schools and teenage pregnancy, violence, and drug use, but do we really believe that the loss of brief morning prayers was the final straw that broke the self-discipline of our children? Ask yourself: Was America a Christian country because of school prayer, or was there school prayer because America was a Christian country? I think the honest answer is that school prayer became an American tradition because it was a true reflection of who we were, or at least who we aspired to be. Our primary battle now is not to retain symbols of a culture that no longer exists. It is, instead, to create a new culture—a new Christian America.

Our children face a desperate battle for their souls. If Columbine taught us anything, it taught us that some of our young people are enmeshed in a darkness so vile that we can scarcely comprehend it. We live in a society that often works overtime to nourish the worst in our souls—with a nonstop media assault on almost every virtue essential to Christian life.

These children need Jesus Christ. They need the Holy Spirit of the Living God. And make no mistake, they do not know Jesus. They barely even know who He is. Consider these vignettes:[19]

- A professor at the University of North Carolina (one of the better public universities in America—located in a Bible Belt state) gave his religion students a quiz of 30 questions on the Bible, Western religious history, and world religions. Nobody got more than 70 percent of the answers correct. The average score was 28 percent. Only 55 percent could name the first two books of the Bible.
- An English teacher in a Massachusetts high school asked five classes of college-bound students 112 questions about biblical stories and characters. Seventy percent were answered incorrectly. Students said that Sodom and Gomorrah were lovers, that Jesus was baptized by Moses, that Jezebel was Ahab's donkey, and that the stories of Jesus were called "parodies."
- A professor at Eastern Washington University surveyed the 60 students in his introductory religion class about their knowledge of the Bible. One-third admitted to knowing nothing about the Bible, its authors, or its contents.

We cannot expect that public school prayer will make even the slightest dent in that vast abyss of ignorance. However, we can be sure that public school prayer will be bitterly resented by a significant number of students, teachers, administrators, and parents. People will be deeply offended—as I would be if my school began each day with a

Wiccan incantation or Muslim prayer. Think for a moment of the golden rule. Would you want a school to require your son or daughter to sit through Buddhist chants? Then why do you want your school to require Buddhist students to sit through Christian prayers? The school prayer movement divides us from the very people we most want to evangelize. School prayer arguments destroy any hope of successfully stopping the leftist indoctrination that is permeating our schools. Government-sponsored public school prayer is a bad idea.

It may be true that America was, at one time, a Christian country. That is no longer true, and school prayer movements cannot make it true. The alternatives to school prayer become obvious when we ask and answer two simple questions: (1) How is the gospel spreading through our public schools? and (2) Which human activities are the greatest threats to the gospel message? The answer to the first question is obvious. As discussed in the previous section, the gospel is spreading because hundreds of thousands of Christians, empowered by the Holy Spirit, are using the freedoms they have left to draw their classmates to Christ. I would submit that the governmental threats to this movement are twofold: a constant attack on Christian freedom accompanied by a steady drumbeat of liberal indoctrination.

The attack on Christian freedom is being effectively countered. The liberal indoctrination is not. My proposal is simple: supplement our message of freedom with an assault on public moral indoctrination—any indoctrination. Our position should be clear and unequivocal. It is not the government's job to teach our children how to live. The government should not favor any particular worldview, and it certainly should not attack specific religions or religion in general. There should be no more public seminars entitled "Religious Wrong," and Christian students should not be mocked at public events.

Although the principle is simple, its execution is not. As I have carefully explained, the Constitution currently allows state-sponsored liberal indoctrination. At the present time, we cannot go to court to shut down Hot, Sexy and Safer Productions. Presently, the courts are not the best forum for our arguments. We cannot rely on lawyers alone. Instead, individual Christians in thousands of local school boards must humbly, lovingly, and courageously ask schools to select more balanced textbooks—books that at least acknowledge that the Pilgrims were Christian or that evolution is still a theory. Christians must ask school boards and state boards of education to turn their back on textbooks and classroom methods that purport to train our children according to a particular worldview. Schools can educate children about religion or about liberalism, but they cannot take that extra step and actually ask us to be liberal or to be religious.

Christian lawyers must remain alert and watchful. While the courts have thus far resoundingly rejected the idea that leftists are violating the establishment clause when they fervently teach values that are incompatible with Christianity, the left is growing bolder. They may go too far, even for a secular judge—and hand us a significant legal victory. At the very least, the knowledge that indoctrination courts litigation will have a chilling effect on those who seek to "reeducate" our Christian youth.

Also, if we want to break the back of public school indoctrination, we should support the voucher system. "Vouchers" are a shorthand reference for various government programs that take a portion of the money that would ordinarily be funneled into public schools and instead distribute those funds directly to parents. The parents are then able to choose whether to spend that money on private school tuition or to put it (and their child) back into the public school system. This program would allow hundreds of thousands of middle-class, lower-middle-class, and poor students to turn their backs on a school system that is failing them.

It is difficult to overstate the revolutionary aspects of the voucher system. Almost overnight, the number of children enrolled in Christian academies and parochial schools (the primary alternative to public schools) would explode, and these children would receive not only a generally higher-quality education but also an unvarnished presentation of the gospel—not from the government but from people who actually *believe.*

Since children would have the freedom to leave failing schools, educational and economic opportunities for some of the poorest, most marginalized members of society would increase substantially. I spent a year on the admissions committee of Cornell Law School, and I have firsthand evidence of the lasting effects of substandard public school education on poor and minority children. Parents without money, without choice or hope, would at a stroke find themselves empowered and able to take control of their children's futures. No longer would children be forced to listen to the government's message. No longer would children be trapped in schools that expend significant resources on condom awareness but graduate entire classes of nearly illiterate students.

White evangelical support for the voucher movement would also help heal breaches with the African-American Christian community. Strong majorities of black parents support vouchers—largely because their children are disproportionately concentrated in America's poorest and worst public schools. While vouchers are largely meaningless to many upper-middle-class whites—who are either happy with their suburban public schools or already able to put their children in private academies—they represent a social and political lifeline to millions of others. Vouchers extend the economic freedom many take for granted to children of all races and social classes.

In short, Christians should stand for freedom. We should stand with people of all religions and backgrounds as they seek a place in the marketplace of ideas. By standing with them, we can reconcile long-standing divisions, and we can open avenues for evangelism. By standing against coercion and tyranny, we will reclaim, once and for all, the moral high ground in the public debate. By supporting educational choice and freedom of expression, we will let other voices be heard, and we will not offend them by forcing them to bow to our God. Remember, only one voice in the marketplace speaks with the power of the Holy Spirit, and the Spirit draws hearts to God—he does not coerce.

4

Dangerous
Christians

A College Attacks Christianity

"God, is the excitement over?"

I asked that question several times during the winter of 2000. I had moved my family from Georgetown, Kentucky, to Ithaca, New York, and life was dull. I had just started teaching at Cornell Law School, and I was getting used to the slow, academic lifestyle.

In Kentucky, I had worked ten, twelve, sometimes fourteen hours a day. Much of my law practice centered on religious freedom. After the dramatic victory discussed in the first chapter of this book, I was literally deluged with calls from Christians needing representation. In the months that followed, I represented Christian individuals, churches, and denominational organizations. It was not unusual for my phone to ring at midnight with frantic questions or tearful pleas for help. Because my Christian clients rarely could pay my normal hourly rate, I had to redouble my efforts in my commercial practice. I worked for a large law firm, and my career depended on the ability to bill at least two thousand hours per year. Representing rural churches was not the ticket to success. So I tried to do it all—represent the small churches and the large companies. By the time we left Kentucky, I was physically exhausted, mentally drained, and spiritually spent.

In Ithaca, the whirlwind was stilled. The phone did not ring, and work—though challenging—was hardly demanding. Often, I would work only during the afternoon or only in the morning. I played with my precious daughter, had three meals a day with my family, and spent my evenings reading, playing tennis, or watching television. I felt like I was on vacation.

I loved my life—for three weeks. Then came the discontent. Was I supposed to live like this? Was life supposed to be this simple and easy? Or had I run from my calling? In Kentucky I knew that we had worked hard for the kingdom, but in Ithaca, I felt that I was living almost purely for myself. I had the job I wanted, a nice apartment, and a wonderful little family. What could be better? And yet . . .

I was bored. The weeks rolled into months, and the boredom deepened into despair. I felt God tugging at my heart, but I did not know what He wanted. Did He want me to be content with the peace and quiet, or did He want me to waken from my slumber? I prayed, and I thought I had begun to discern an answer. The roller-coaster life I had lived was over, and it was time for stability. I was no longer on the front lines of the culture wars. I had classes to teach and a tennis game to perfect.

Then, one afternoon, I checked my E-mail. It was early April 2000. One of my best friends, John Kingston, a Harvard classmate and a thoughtful Christian, wrote and told me that he had two friends at Tufts University who might need legal counsel. His message was singularly uninformative. He simply gave me their phone number and told me that they might need my religious freedom expertise.

Later that afternoon I called the home of Curtis and Jody Chang. Both Curtis and Jody were staff workers for InterVarsity Christian Fellowship. Curtis was the leader of InterVarsity's Boston area "Red Team," given responsibility for the InterVarsity fellowships at Tufts, Harvard, and MIT. Curtis, a Harvard graduate, is a Taiwanese immigrant and one of the most intelligent people I have ever met. He combines an encyclopedic memory with keen analytical skills. He is one of those rare individuals who is both intellectually gifted and has a truly down-to-earth manner and sensibility. He loves baseball and military history, is blessed with a quick wit and a compassionate heart, and possesses an absolute commitment to the gospel.

Jody, his wife, was the most senior InterVarsity staff worker at Tufts. Jody is a true rarity—a Texan with no discernible Southern accent. She shares her husband's intelligence and commitment. Every time I spoke with her, I was impressed with her selflessness. If there was one person who suffered most from the slings and arrows of the enemy in the entire battle that followed, it was Jody Chang. Yet she endured it all with a loving and cheerfully defiant heart.

I spoke to Jody first. I could almost feel the tension and concern in her voice as she told me her story. Jody worked with the Tufts Christian Fellowship (TCF), the oldest and largest evangelical Christian student group at Tufts University.[1] Three years before, a young freshman named Julie Catalano had joined the group. Her background was in the United Churches of Christ, one of the most liberal (and least evangelical) denominations in America, but she seemed enthusiastic about InterVarsity. Within months TCF students and staff workers looked at her as a leader.

Jody described Julie as "hungry" for God, but Julie also seemed troubled. During her freshman year she revealed to several trusted students that she struggled with her sexual orientation and asked for prayer. She spoke to Jody about her concerns, and Jody prayed with her and gave her an InterVarsity Press book about homosexuality.

Although Julie told the group that she sometimes considered herself lesbian or bisexual, she also said that she believed the Bible was clear about proper sexual practice and vowed that she would not "experiment" sexually. Instead, she would continue to pray and seek God. Many TCF students admired Julie's honesty and courage in dealing with a difficult personal issue. She was asked to lead Bible study groups and even led a women's accountability and prayer group. By the middle of her junior year, Julie was recognized as one of TCF's most respected members, and she was a prime candidate for senior leadership.

However, by that time, Julie had begun to change some of her beliefs. Early in the spring semester of her junior year, Julie approached Jody and told her that things had changed. She still believed the Bible was the Word of God, but she did not believe that the Bible prohibited homosexual sex. Julie told Jody that she believed she could date and even marry another woman, so long as she behaved in the same manner as a godly heterosexual couple—saving sex until marriage. This change concerned Jody greatly. Jody and virtually all of TCF's members shared the traditional evangelical view of human sexuality—that sexual intercourse was reserved for the covenant marriage of a man and a woman. Julie now stated her disagreement with this basic principle. Then Julie went even further. She declared that she wanted to apply for senior leadership at TCF, and she wanted assurances from Jody that her new beliefs regarding sexuality would not be considered by TCF during the leadership selection process.

Jody gave a careful response. TCF senior leaders were not selected democratically. It was the responsibility of each year's senior leadership team, after prayer and consultation with TCF members, to select their successors. Jody told Julie that she and the senior leaders would have to consider Julie's new beliefs regarding sexuality during the selection process, but Jody also said that she could not predict what the senior leaders would ultimately decide. The decision was up to the senior leaders, not her.

Julie was enraged by this response. She accused TCF of discriminating against her on the basis of her sexual orientation and filed a formal complaint against TCF. Jody filed a brief written response and denied that TCF was discriminating against Julie. TCF had long known Julie's sexual orientation and had welcomed her as a member and a leader. Instead, TCF was simply exercising basic religious freedom—using religious criteria (interpretation of biblical passages) to select the leaders of a religious organization. As of the day of my first phone call, there had been no hearing on Julie's discrimination complaint, and no hearing had been scheduled.

As I listened to Jody's account, I grew increasingly concerned. In today's politically correct campus environment, Christians often are mocked and ostracized. At the same time, gay students have achieved increasing levels of prominence and power. When I was at Harvard Law School, the school chapter of the Lambda Legal Defense Fund, a gay and lesbian legal organization, was one of the most militant, active organizations on campus. Individuals who criticized gays or gay rights policies sometimes found their faces plastered over gay pornography and posted on bulletin boards around the school. To be called "homophobic" was an insult equal to being called "racist" or "sexist."

Moreover, gay interests are often vigilantly protected by school policies and departments. Many universities have implemented speech codes that prohibit speech that is "discriminatory" or "offensive" to gays and lesbians. Other universities have passed sweeping anti-discrimination policies that prohibit discrimination on the basis of race, sex, ethnicity, or sexual orientation.

Even worse for TCF, I knew that Tufts was a private university. Consequently, TCF actions were not protected by the First Amendment's free exercise clause. The Constitution does not protect individuals or groups against private behavior. The Constitution restrains government action only. This is a surprising reality to most Americans, who are trained almost from birth to believe that they have Constitutional rights in almost every conceivable situation. However, it is a reality that Christians must understand. Private organizations are, to a large extent, free to formulate their own policies and, often, free to exclude or marginalize Christians. If Tufts wanted to ban Christians from its campus, the Constitution would not stop it.

However, TCF was not helpless. If the Constitution did not protect TCF, Massachusetts laws might. Most states hold that student handbooks are contracts between the school and the student. Just as the student is required to follow the school's policies, so is the school. If Tufts guaranteed religious freedom or free association rights, then TCF's case would be infinitely stronger.

I tried to explain these facts to Jody and asked her to send me Tufts' student handbooks and discipline manuals. My plan was simple: I would review the manuals, research Massachusetts law, and then contact the Tufts administration and try to ensure that TCF had a fair opportunity to make its case.

The first step was to learn as much as I could about the university. Tufts is one of America's elite universities, consistently ranked among the top twenty-five national liberal arts universities by *U.S. News and World Report*. Like most secular universities, Tufts trumpets its commitment to diversity. A quick glance at the university's Web site reveals that Tufts is the home of a multinational, diverse student body. Student groups proliferate. There are groups dedicated to political and cultural causes and groups dedicated to race or religion. The list seems endless: The Pan-African Alliance; the Tufts Transgendered, Lesbian, Gay, Bisexual Collective; Hillel; the Latino Student Center; the Tufts Armenian Club; the Hellenic Society; and many others.

Tufts has an Office of Diversity and several official "centers" that promote the interests of African-Americans; Asian-Americans; Latinos and Latinas; Women; and Gays, Lesbians, and Bisexuals. To complement these various centers and to ensure that Tufts provides a "welcoming" environment for its students and faculty, the university has implemented a sweeping antidiscrimination policy. The university, faculty members, and even student groups are prohibited from discriminating on the basis of race, religion, ethnicity, disability, sexual orientation, nationality, and a host of other categories. Additionally, the university prohibits several forms of "harassment," including harassment based on sexual orientation. After surveying these policies, I knew that TCF faced a daunting challenge.

But it was a challenge that had to be met. My description of Tufts could also stand as a description of virtually every elite secular university in this country. If Christians were to maintain a presence in the Ivy League, or in secular higher education in general, we would have to find a way to keep TCF alive—and free.

A Midnight Meeting

I awoke early the morning of Friday, April 14. I am an avid baseball fan, and I belong to a fantasy baseball league comprised of sixteen friends from law school and elsewhere. Each year, we gather in Boston or Washington, D.C., for our annual draft. Draft 2000 was to be held in Boston. Draft festivities would begin early Friday evening, and I was looking forward not just to seeing old friends but also to meeting Curtis Chang, my new client and, coincidentally, our baseball league's newest member.

I was packing to leave when the phone rang. It was Jody. She sounded shocked and angry. "We've been banned," she said.

"What? Banned? What happened?"

"The Judiciary [the Tufts Community Union Judiciary that heard Julie Catalano's complaint] met late last night—without us even there—and voted to derecognize us. We've been kicked off campus! We got a message on our answering machine sometime after midnight telling us about the meeting and the decision."

My mind was racing. I found it difficult to believe that TCF could be thrown off campus before it even had an opportunity to defend itself. I had just barely started my review of Tufts policies. "How can they do this? Don't we get a hearing? I thought we were entitled to a hearing."

"I thought we were too, but evidently the 'J' [Tufts terminology for the Judiciary] can act without a hearing when they believe that the safety of the community is at stake."

"The safety of the community? You've got to be kidding me!" I thought I had become accustomed to the liberal tendency to exaggerate the dangers of conservative and Christian thought—to label us as "Nazis" or "fascists"—but this surprised even me. How could TCF threaten the safety of the Tufts community?

"That's right. There was a speaker on campus last night, and Julie's complaint came up. Evidently, she said that TCF had made her feel suicidal, and that caused a pretty big reaction. Anyway, the J met without us and just threw us off campus. We've got our regularly scheduled meeting tonight, but we can't meet on campus."

"OK. What exactly does it mean to be derecognized?"

I could tell that Jody was extremely upset by the J's maneuver, but she was speaking with remarkable clarity. "It means that we lose our funding, we can't reserve rooms on campus, we can't advertise on campus, and we can't participate in the annual student activities fair. I talked to an administrator and asked exactly what it meant, and she said, 'Basically, as far as Tufts is concerned, you don't exist.'"

I had recovered from my initial surprise, and I was feeling angry—and determined. "If you can get me the phone number for the university's

General Counsel, I'll call and see what we need to do to appeal this decision. If the student handbook says we get a hearing, then we get a hearing. If they don't let us have that hearing, then they're breaking the law. See if you can talk to the dean of students to see if he'll give you any information. I'll be in Boston by 6:00 P.M. I'd love to see you or Curtis then. Give me everything you've got. I'll need Julie's complaint, your response, any student newspaper accounts of this meeting, appeal procedures—everything."

Jody agreed to gather what she could, and we ended the conversation. I then called the university's General Counsel. Their office was closed, so I left a polite, but firm message: "Hello, this is David French from Cornell Law School. I represent the Tufts Christian Fellowship. I understand that the J met last night and voted, without holding an actual hearing, to ban TCF from campus. I don't understand how that action could be procedurally proper. Please contact me at your earliest convenience." I left my contact information then departed for Boston.

I was not able to meet with Curtis until midnight Friday. By the end of our conversation, I began to realize the magnitude of Tufts' mistake. The enemy had launched a frontal attack on campus Christianity, but God had raised up a legion of warriors to oppose him. By the time I saw Curtis, he had already typed up a comprehensive defense of TCF's position. He planned to submit this defense not only to the Tufts student newspaper but also to local and national media outlets. As I read this defense, and as I talked to Curtis, I learned even more about the case.

TCF had not told Julie that she could not become a senior leader because she was gay. Nor had their consideration of the question been a mere formality. The senior leaders had met several times to pray about the issue, and they were all tormented by their decision. The senior leaders invited a liberal Christian pastor to present the view that the Bible did not prohibit homosexual sexual activity. They prayed even more. Each of the senior leaders loved Julie deeply, but, ultimately, they could not compromise their view of biblical truth even for someone they loved. It did not matter to them that Julie felt that her "orientation" was lesbian, but it did matter to them that Julie no longer intended to abide by clear, scriptural commands. Even though they knew that their decision would result in campus ridicule and public persecution, they had voted unanimously against Julie's leadership application.

High Stakes

As I reviewed our legal options, Curtis began a one-man media crusade. He faxed press releases to local newspapers and national media outlets. Within days of the J's midnight meeting, news reports surfaced in the *Washington Times* and the *Boston Herald.* As news of the case spread, we became aware of other Christian fellowships at other colleges that were experiencing the same kind of persecution. Fellowship groups at Middlebury College in Vermont, Williams College in Massachusetts, Ball State University in Indiana, Whitman College in Washington, and Grinnell College in Iowa faced discrimination complaints, administration sanctions, and even outright bans.

Put simply, TCF found itself on the front edge of a new wave of religious persecution: the use of antidiscrimination rules to vilify and punish conservative Christian organizations. Antidiscrimination regulations can be almost perfect vehicles for religious persecution. They are often initially enacted for the purest of motives. Activists claim only to want to protect historically disadvantaged groups from oppression. "No one," they argue, "should be denied a job, or a place at a university, or membership in a club, simply because they are [black, or a woman, or a veteran, or disabled, or gay]." Antidiscrimination provisions are not enacted to defeat religion; they are enacted to protect people from prejudice or bigotry. Most Americans enthusiastically support those goals, and if you raise a voice in protest, you are often accused of racism, sexism, classism, or homophobia.

However, these antidiscrimination statutes come with a price. When antidiscrimination rules protect people from discrimination on the basis of race, most evangelicals cheer. We support using the power of government to help erase the legacy of racism and slavery. However, the regulations are not limited to race. When gender, sexual orientation, and even religion are thrown into the mix (as they are at Tufts), then life can become difficult for religious individuals and can become groups.

It is obvious that the Bible itself "discriminates" on the basis of gender and sexual orientation. In other words, God has "discriminated" (a loaded synonym for simply making choices) by choosing men as the heads of households and reserving sexual activity for covenant marriages between a man and a woman. Since God has discriminated, we Christians then discriminate when we apply those principles—principles that we believe give life and hope—to our lives and our churches. When we say that we do not want a student group to be led by an openly gay individual, we are discriminating on two bases—religion and sexual orientation.

Christians are not alone in their "discrimination." Muslims and conservative and orthodox Jews are sometimes even more emphatic in their denunciation of homosexual behavior or in their declaration of specific gender roles. If antidiscrimination rules were applied to their institutions, the results would be catastrophic. Quite literally, antidiscrimination rules, if applied universally, can destroy the sanctity of the mosque, the synagogue, and the church. If we cannot use our religious principles to guide our decisions, then we are not a religious people.

At Tufts, the battle lines were clear. It was the irresistible force against the immovable object. The antidiscrimination movement and liberal protective politics were in direct conflict with religious freedom and freedom of expression. One side would win, and the other side would lose. There was no middle ground.

From the outset, both sides realized the stakes. On 29 April 2000, the *Boston Globe* ran a major story on the problems faced by Christian campus organizations. Elliott Abrams, former assistant secretary of state for human rights, made our point perfectly: "What Tufts and Middlebury are really saying is that the view that the Bible takes is an illegitimate view, and you can get thrown off campus for it. That's bigotry. The message being sent by these schools to evangelicals is, 'If you're really serious about your beliefs, why don't you go to Bob Jones University and not here?'"[2]

The gay lobby's response was also a perfect expression of their principles. "They should abide by the nondiscrimination policies of the universities," argued David Smith, communications director for the Human Rights Campaign, a prominent gay rights group. "It's our belief that religion should never be used to justify discrimination against gay people in public settings."[3] Stated another way, as a precondition to participating in the public life of a campus or of a nation, religious people must abandon their religious principles.

Our response to this argument was simple. If you banned the Tufts Christian Fellowship for applying religious principles to religious decisions, then you destroyed freedom for everyone—not just TCF. If it is improper for TCF to require its leaders to be evangelical Christians, how would it be proper for gay rights groups to require their leaders to support gay rights, or for leaders of Jewish groups not to be anti-Semitic members of Hamas? If every group must include everyone and be led by everyone, then there is no true diversity—no difference. There is only the crushing sameness of the Tufts-approved ideology.

Additionally, TCF was not trying to argue that Julie Catalano should be kicked off campus or that there should not be a vibrant gay community at Tufts. In fact, Tufts' diversity was one of the reasons why many of TCF's students chose to attend the school in the first place. TCF just wanted to be a part of that community. We wanted the right to advertise our existence, meet in empty classrooms, and share the gospel of Jesus Christ. We did not care about student funding. Numerous times throughout the dispute, we offered to give up our share of the student activity fee (Curtis—inspired by the biblical admonition that if an "enemy asks for your shirt, give him your cloak as well"—even proposed giving TCF's funds to the Tufts Transgendered, Lesbian, Gay, Bisexual Collective) so long as we had the opportunity to meet and speak. Those offers were rejected. TCF's speech was too dangerous—too "unsafe"—to be heard.

The Media War

Soon after the *Boston Globe* story, the media battle began to heat up. Curtis's faxes had touched a nerve, and calls came pouring in. A Boston public television station broadcast a debate between Julie Catalano and a member of TCF's senior leadership. (In an interesting display of PBS bias, Julie was shuttled to and from the broadcast in a limousine while TCF's representative had to find his own way to the station.) As the intensity increased, Curtis made a critical decision. He called for help.

In hindsight, I can clearly see how God's hand guided Curtis through the early days of the crisis. Every move he made was perfect. His comments were clear, courageous, and compassionate. The press accounts that followed were remarkably evenhanded and often favorable to TCF. God's providence was also evident in Curtis's appeal for help—and in the response to that appeal.

Curtis reached out to the Foundation for Individual Rights in Education (FIRE), a relatively new organization dedicated to halting the tidal wave of politically correct orthodoxy that is sweeping higher education. They are civil libertarians in the truest sense of the word— firm believers that education is enriched when we all have a place in the marketplace of ideas. FIRE represents students who are denied due process rights, teachers whose words are censored by the P.C. cadres, and student groups that stand outside the ideological mainstream of modern secular education. FIRE is an implacable opponent of speech codes, secret proceedings, overbroad antiharassment guidelines, and political repression of all kinds. Because FIRE is not Christian and because it is neither liberal nor conservative, it speaks with a voice that is not easy for the elite media to dismiss.

FIRE firmly believes the words of Justice Louis Brandeis: "Sunlight is the best disinfectant." Put another way, "The darkness hates the light." FIRE, working with Curtis, put a spotlight on the J's midnight meeting and on the administration's disingenuous posturing. FIRE representatives were quoted in article after article and, within days, prominent national commentators began to weigh in on TCF's case.

John Leo, a respected conservative commentator for *U.S. News & World Report,* wrote an article decrying the J's decision. Other conservative columnists, like Cal Thomas and Jeff Jacoby, followed suit. William Bennett, former Secretary of Education and author of the *Book of Virtues,* penned an editorial that was submitted to several national newspapers. *ABC News* contacted Curtis and began discussing the possibility of a lengthy report from the Tufts campus. Simultaneously, FIRE circulated a petition among prominent academics, demanding that TCF be reinstated.

While Curtis and FIRE were tasked with media relations, I toiled in relative obscurity, focusing on the relevant legal issues. However, I was not immune from the media storm. At the height of the struggle, I received no less than five calls per day. Sometimes I was quoted directly, but more often I provided background information, trying to frame the legal issues in a way that the reporters would understand.

The legal issues were both simple and complicated. The J—by holding a secret, midnight meeting—had clearly violated our due process rights. Tufts' discipline codes provided that every accused student or student group had a right to be heard, unless the allegation was not disputed. Because we disputed Julie Catalano's claims, we were entitled to a hearing. It was that simple.

Our arguments at that hearing—if we ever got a hearing—would be much more complex. Tufts policies were a confusing mishmash of rules and rhetoric. The Tufts student handbook stated that it was the "educational policy" of the university not to discriminate on the basis of religion. Also, the rules governing Tufts' student groups stated that Tufts protected "freedom of association." However, those same rules then stated that no student group could discriminate on the basis of race, religion, gender, sexual orientation, and so on. In other words, this expansive antidiscrimination policy eviscerated freedom of association. As near as I could tell, Tufts protected religious freedom only as long as its students did not actually practice their religion.

When I drafted TCF's appeal, I focused on the simple argument. The J's ruling was improper because we never had an opportunity to be heard. Our plan was to attempt to reverse the J's decision on procedural grounds then spend the summer attempting to reach a resolution that would avoid the necessity for further hearings.

We made our appeal when the public pressure was at its peak. FIRE's petition reached the administration within days of the appeal board's hearing. Also, Curtis and FIRE had begun contacting Tufts' alums, seeking to open a new avenue of persuasion. Tufts' counsel expressed alarm at the level of publicity and asked me to curtail FIRE's activities. He said that the appeal board was in "serious discussion" and that any further publicity would only "complicate" the issues. Although

I sympathized with his predicament, there was no way that we were decreasing the pressure. The J's decision had been made in secret, but the appeal board was operating under a national spotlight.

On Monday, May 15, we received the appeal board's ruling. The J's illegal action was reversed, and TCF was reinstated. The *Boston Globe* described the decision:

> At Tufts, the student-faculty Committee on Student Life voted unanimously Monday to reinstate the Tufts Christian Fellowship . . . the Committee on Student Life ruled that the student judiciary violated due process rights of the evangelical Christians by not holding a hearing before issuing its decision. The committee recommended that the student judiciary hold another hearing, presumably in the fall when students return.[4]

We had won . . . temporarily. While TCF's seniors would be able to graduate not as criminal outcasts, but as members of a recognized student organization, the group's ultimate fate was still undecided. While TCF celebrated its victory, my thoughts turned to the fall and the coming hearing. "This is far from over," warned a Tufts spokeswoman. "It's definitely going to come up again, and the issue of discrimination is still unresolved."[5] Gay rights advocates vowed not to let the matter drop. Judith Brown, director of Tufts' Lesbian Gay Bisexual Transgender Center, was clear. "We will not leave this matter behind. Student groups should have to abide by the university's nondiscrimination policy."[6]

Curtis and Jody's courage, FIRE's tenacity, and, above all, God's grace brought us victory on the first part of our plan. But there was one more battle to be fought—a battle for ultimate survival before the same group that banned us once before.

5

The Post-Christian College

The Indoctrination, Intimidation, and Exclusion of Campus Christians

The story of Tufts Christian Fellowship presents the perfect backdrop to a more general discussion of the challenges faced by evangelical Christians in America's elite colleges and universities. Too often, we shake our heads at the latest examples of "P.C. excess" or administrative hate-mongering while forgetting that individual Christians—our children—are being crushed, marginalized, and excluded. To us, academic arguments and extreme identity politics are merely ridiculous. To our children, they are a daily, soul-destroying challenge.

Without thinking, and with a fraction of the parental involvement and political attention we invest in public secondary schools, we send our children into a lion's den infinitely more challenging, infinitely more dangerous than a hundred "Hot, Sexy and Safer" assemblies. We invest, collectively, tens of thousands of hours fighting for ritualistic football game prayer and almost no time even thinking about how many of America's best colleges are essentially in the business of rooting out Christianity and Christian influence from the academy, from business, from government, and—most important—from your children.

When you hear about the bigotry at Tufts, it may seem distant. After all, the controversy there impacted no more than fifty Christian students. "Besides," you think, "I don't even know anyone who attends Tufts. I've never even heard of Tufts." Or maybe you think that Tufts is one of those "liberal" Northeastern schools, the kind of place that you gave up worrying about long ago. Your kids go somewhere more conservative, more conventional—someplace more sane.

Yet, increasingly, there is no place more sane. In the midst of the Tufts controversy, InterVarsity Christian Fellowship created a "Religious Freedom Crisis Team." InterVarsity, with its national and international network of student fellowships, knew that TCF's dilemma was hardly unique. Every year, university administrations move against Christians and Christian groups. InterVarsity needed to respond to these crises.

During the 2000–2001 school year, I served as the Crisis Team's Chief Legal Counsel. Within six months I had worked with Christian fellowships at public and private schools in Vermont, Massachusetts, New York, Iowa, Washington, California, Indiana, and Florida. In virtually every case the administration was threatening to ban evangelical Christian groups from campus. Also in every case the reason for the ban was the group's alleged "discriminatory" policies. At two public universities the administration even threatened to ban Christian groups that insisted on "discriminating" on the basis of religion. In other words, in the view of these schools, it was improper for a Christian student organization to insist that it be run by Christians.

It is vital that America's Christian public understand what is happening. In the first major section of this book, I described how the current legal structure is unbalanced—weighted in favor of religiously zealous liberals and against Christians. One consequence of that unbalanced playing field is a public school system that permitted, and sometimes even encouraged, the teaching of moral doctrines that directly opposed Christianity.

This lack of balance is alarming not only because of what public schools actually are but also because of what they might become. The vast majority of public school systems are not yet hotbeds of radical leftist thought. They are, more often, small-scale reflections of their community—radically liberal in places like Ithaca, New York, and solidly conservative in Paris, Tennessee. Most Christians have written off Ithaca. The fight is to preserve Paris.

With respect to America's major educational institutions, there is no Paris. A generations-long assault on conservatism, religion, and freedom has led to the creation of an educational structure that is truly post-Christian. If one wants to see what our public high schools might become, simply take a long tour of a major state university, or of virtually any private, secular college. In other words, for our Christian children, the move from public high school to college is a move from a moderately warm frying pan into a raging fire.

In this section of the book, I will examine how, for many Christians, the secular college experience is often characterized by three experiences: reeducation, intimidation, and exclusion. My arguments are drawn not only from my own education but also from the accumulated experiences of tens of thousands—experiences that are documented in an increasing number of books, magazines, and academic journals.

Reeducation

I have vivid memories of my freshman orientation. As I have mentioned, I attended David Lipscomb University, a small Christian college in Nashville, Tennessee. My father had gone to Lipscomb; my mother had gone to Lipscomb; my grandfather was a Lipscomb graduate; and many of my aunts, uncles, and cousins either graduated from Lipscomb or currently attended. In short, "Bison" blood ran in my veins.

Growing up, I was surrounded by stories of the "Lipscomb experience," and some of the fondest memories revolved around freshman orientation. Freshmen arrived at campus early and spent almost a full week getting to know one another. There were no classes and no homework assignments. Instead, the days were filled with "mixers" and the nights with (proper, nonraucous) parties and midnight devotionals. We played silly games, met potential dates, and began lifelong friendships. Lipscomb, like many colleges, is a place steeped in traditions, and a joyful, playful orientation is one of its best.

Lipscomb, however, is not your typical college. Those students who do not choose Christian colleges often face a very different reality. Their first days of college are not filled with lighthearted activities. Instead, they face the first, grim round of indoctrination. From their first moments on campus, they are taught to abandon the faith and beliefs of their parents, their community, and their church. The radical left commences its proselytization.

In the March 2000 issue of *Reason* magazine, Alan Charles Kors, the president of the Foundation for Individual Rights in Education and the coauthor of *The Shadow University,* a meticulously documented examination and critique of campus political correctness, published an article called "Thought Reform 101."[1] The article explored the changing nature of campus orientation programs and related several sobering examples of ideological reeducation.

At Wake Forest University, students were required to attend "Blue Eyed," a racism awareness workshop "in which whites are abused, ridiculed, made to fail, and taught helpless passivity so that they can identify with a 'person of color' for the day." Columbia University's orientation is designed to give students the chance to "'reevaluate [and] learn things,' so that they could rid themselves of 'their own social and personal beliefs that foster inequality.'" Professor Kors's report is startling. His research revealed that "at almost all of our campuses, some form of moral and political reeducation has been built into freshman orientation and residential programming. These exercises have become so commonplace that most students do not even think of the issues of privacy, rights, and dignity involved."

It is simply a fact that a freshman entering a secular American college is likely to be taught, from the very first day of his college experience, that much of what he previously learned or understood about race, gender, sexuality, and even religion is simply wrong. But he will be taught that he (or his parents) were more than just wrong. He will be told that he is steeped in racism, sexism, classism, and homophobia. He often will be required to "confess" his sins and the sins of his parents. Students from small-town or conservative backgrounds will be expected to "grow" and embrace "diversity" and "tolerance."

It is difficult to overestimate how much this intrudes upon the identities and values of many Christians. The Christian who truly believes that, in Christ, there is "no man, no woman, no Jew, no Gentile, no slave, no free," but that we are all "one in Christ Jesus" (Gal. 3:28, author's paraphrase), will find that his message of unity is scorned and must fall before the altar of identity politics. The Christian who believes that sexual behavior is properly reserved for a covenant marriage between a man and woman will find that his views are not just mocked as "backward" or "nerdy" but reviled as hateful or homophobic. Student facilitators and administrators will make intensive efforts to change the Christian's heart.

Professor Kors indicts these programs with a powerful analogy:

> The darkest nightmare of the literature on power is
> George Orwell's *1984,* where there is not even an inte-
> rior space of privacy and self. Winston Smith faces the
> ultimate and consistent logic of the argument that
> everything is political, and he can only dream of "a time
> when there were still privacy, love, and friendship, and
> when members of a family stood by one another with-
> out needing to know the reason." Orwell did not know
> that as he wrote, Mao's China was subjecting university
> students to "thought reform" . . . that was not complete
> until children had denounced the lives and political
> morals of their parents and emerged as "progressive" in a
> manner satisfactory to their trainers. In the diversity
> education film *Skin Deep,* a favorite in academic "sensi-
> tivity training," a white student in his third day of a
> "facilitated" retreat on race, with his name on the screen
> and his college and hometown identified, confesses his
> family's inertial Southern racism and, catching his
> breath, says to the group (and to the thousands of stu-
> dents who will see this film on their own campuses),
> "It's a tough choice, choosing what's right and choosing
> your family."[2]

While modern campus orientations are hardly as coercive as Mao's
reeducation camps, it is important to realize the truth of what's happening. America's public and private colleges have taken it upon themselves to teach your children a particular worldview—a worldview that
is diametrically opposed to much of the Bible. These colleges will
require your children to listen to this teaching, and they will often

require your children to participate actively in tolerance-themed teaching activities.

This indoctrination does not end with freshman orientation. It extends into virtually every day of every academic year of a student's college experience. The Christian student can expect to be surrounded by students whose views of Christianity range from apathy to hostility, and, more important, a Christian student can expect *never* to take a class taught by a Christian teacher.

When I was at Harvard—after spending four years at a Christian school—I was surprised by both the unrelenting liberalism of my professors and by their daily zeal in advancing their various worldviews. I had a charismatic, popular contracts professor who used his class as a launching pad for a "critical legal studies" attack on the racism, classism, sexism, and homophobia of the dominant "white male patriarchy." I had a civil procedure teacher who spent fully one-third of the class talking about the impact of mundane procedural rules on women and minorities. My torts professor had a similar theme, and much of my criminal law class was an exercise in coercing a reexamination of our attitudes towards race and poverty. My property professor was the only first-year instructor who did not exhibit any discernible ideological bias.

Things did not improve as I progressed through school. My family law professors tried to persuade their students to abandon traditional conceptions of childhood, gender, and parental roles. My human rights teacher spent much of the class attacking religious fundamentalism of all stripes, and my corporations professor tried to get us to see the oppression inherent in Delaware corporate law. My educational experience was capped off by a vigorous argument with Alan Dershowitz (my ethics professor) over whether Christian judges should recuse themselves from any consideration of abortion or other moral issues because they are "biased." In three years of law school, I did not have a single

Christian professor, and I did not have a single professor that any reasonable person would consider even remotely conservative. My best professors were liberals who gave conservatives a respectful hearing.

Harvard is not unique. Five years after graduation, I left the private practice of law for a two-year teaching stint at Cornell Law School. Toward the end of my final semester, one of my students stopped by my office and asked me if I knew of any pro-life professors at the law school. He knew that I was leaving, and he wondered if there was anyone else who could mentor him as he wrote a major paper from a pro-life perspective. I told him that I could not think of any other pro-life professors, but I promised that I would investigate the question and get back to him. I asked around the faculty and shortly discovered that, to the best of anyone's knowledge, I was the only pro-life teacher at the school. In other words, the "diverse" faculty that Cornell often boasted of did not feature a single professor, tenured or nontenured, who deviated from the proabortion line.

During my last year at Cornell, I was invited to speak at a symposium entitled "Teaching Ethics in a Pluralist Society." The symposium was sponsored by the Cornell Christian Faculty/Staff Forum, a small group comprised of Christian professors at Cornell's various colleges and schools. Cornell was initiating a new ethics curriculum, and the small band of Christian professors was concerned that the Judeo-Christian worldview was being shut out of the discussion. During the symposium it was revealed that some of Cornell's most prestigious, influential departments had not hired a single Christian—or even a single conservative—in more than a decade. In those departments—like philosophy, government, and other subjects in the humanities—where ideology mattered a great deal, the Christian presence was almost nonexistent. Those Christian professors whom I did know tended to be concentrated in the sciences, where hard research could still (occasionally) trump religious prejudice.

And it's not just faculties that are ideological monoliths. The students of most elite universities are as relentlessly liberal as their professors. When I was at Harvard, I was booed and hissed countless times as I expressed rather conventional Christian or conservative ideas. In my first-year section of approximately 140 students, less than ten could be considered conservative. By the end of the first month of classes, most of them hardly ever spoke in class—cowed into silence by their classmates.

On more than one occasion—after particularly sharp classroom exchanges—I was approached by classmates who told me that they had never actually met an evangelical Christian. Often, those observations triggered interesting conversations (like the one described in chapter 2). More often, however, my classmates never even tried to engage me on a personal level. To this day, one of my classmates—who happened to work with a close Christian friend—has to be persuaded by that friend that I am not a hateful, racist bigot! He reached that conclusion based on a series of constitutional law classes where I argued against race-based affirmative action and in favor of class-based affirmative action—an idea that would still disproportionately benefit blacks, Latinos, and other historically disadvantaged minorities.

My Cornell students were often described by fellow faculty members as "disappointingly moderate." I was amazed. Outside of a few Christians, I did not meet a single student who espoused pro-life or other socially conservative views. To be sure, most of my students embraced capitalism wholeheartedly—law firm salaries were exploding, after all—but a rejection of Marxism hardly makes one "moderate."

During the 2000 election, I set aside an entire class period to discuss the legal issues presented by the various Florida ballot controversies. Within minutes, it became apparent that the class was revolted by George W. Bush and wholeheartedly supported Gore's legal efforts. I had originally planned to try to present both sides of the argument in as evenhanded manner as possible. When not a single student spoke up in favor of Bush, I abandoned any pretense of impartiality and threw myself behind Bush. At one point, I asked for a show of hands of students who supported Bush, Gore, or Nader. Not a single student identified himself as a Bush supporter. Instead, the class was split into sizable Gore and Nader camps.

While I will not pretend that my experience constitutes a comprehensive, scholarly examination of student and faculty political attitudes, it is most certainly relevant and informative. Harvard and Cornell are not educational backwaters. Together, they represent two of the top ten law schools and top ten colleges in the United States. I challenge any person to show me that any one of the rest of the top ten is substantially different. If you extend the analysis to the top twenty or top thirty, the result will hardly be different (at the time of the TCF controversy, *U.S. News & World Report* ranked Tufts as the twenty-fifth best national university). I can state with the utmost confidence that a Christian student at virtually any major national university will almost never hear his worldview promoted or endorsed. If he is fortunate, his ideas will be occasionally tolerated. In general, he will be subjected to an intense, sometimes intimidating and frightening effort by administrators, teachers, and fellow students to "educate" him out of evangelical Christianity.

Intimidation

When I was a first-year law student, I joined Harvard's chapter of the Rutherford Institute. As I've described previously, the Rutherford Institute is a national legal organization that advocates religious freedom and the rights of the unborn. Although Rutherford Institute attorneys have represented individuals from a variety of religions, it is typically considered a Christian legal organization. Most recently, the

Institute gained national notoriety when its founder, John Whitehead, represented Paula Jones in her sexual harassment suit against Bill Clinton.

At Harvard, the student chapter was tiny. During my first year, only five or six individuals—out of a total student population that exceeded 1,700—attended the meetings. To our shame, we did almost nothing. The group was essentially on life support. We helped local attorneys with religious freedom cases (like the "Hot, Sexy and Safer" case discussed in chapter 3), and we would send out an annual letter to the student body regarding Harvard's elective abortion financing policies. That was just about all we did.

My first year, I offered to write the "abortion letter." The abortion letter contained a very straightforward description of one aspect of Harvard's abortion policy. Every student was required to pay a health services fee of several hundred dollars. This fee (essentially an insurance payment) covered the cost of student medical care at Harvard. Harvard's medical facilities performed elective abortions, and those abortions were completely paid for by the health services fee. Under university policy, a student who had moral objections to abortion could write the university and request a refund of that portion of their fee that traditionally had been used to pay for elective abortions. The refund was never more than a few cents, but we believed that it had important symbolic purpose.

I wrote a letter describing Harvard's policy and describing the refund opportunity. At the end of the letter, I attached a short form. If a student wanted an abortion-related refund, they merely had to fill out the form and return it to my campus mailbox. I would forward the forms to the appropriate university office. The letter was relatively brief and—I thought—rather dry and uninspiring.

The morning after I distributed the letter, I saw that my mailbox was jammed with responses. For a moment my heart soared—until I actually read the forms themselves. The first form was blunt enough: "Die, you_____ fascist pig!" The next contained an even more concise "_____ you!" In all, less than a third of the responses were actual refund requests. The rest were vicious, often profanity-laced tirades against me personally, the Rutherford Institute, prolife activists, and/or the "religious right." Not one of the opposing notes contained even a trace of a comprehensible argument against the position we took in the letter. Instead, the responses were a collective demand that we shut up—or suffer ridicule, violence, or death.

These hate messages were my introduction to political "discourse" at Harvard. While my professors and many of my classmates sought to educate me out of my beliefs—a practice I found relentless but non-threatening—other classmates simply attempted to intimidate me into silence. I was booed, hissed, and mocked. Sometimes a student would cry out while I asked a question or made a statement—attempting to drown out the sound of my voice.

My favorite example of classroom intimidation came in my Child, Family, and the State class. The discussion centered on the legality and morality of in vitro fertilization, and the discussion veered naturally toward abortion. The professor then began disparaging antichoice activists who loved "clumps of cells" more than real, live women. She then proceeded to refer to unborn children not as fetuses or embryos (the media's favorite words) but as "biologic product."

I raised my hand. The professor promptly called on me. My comment was relatively simple: "I'd like to object to the terminology used in this discussion. I think it's an interesting example of how word choice and language are used to manipulate opinions. Antiabortion activists are not 'antichoice.' In fact, they favor a lot of choices and personal freedoms. They simply do not believe that a person should have the 'choice' to take the life of another human being. If you don't want to call them prolife—because you don't believe an unborn child is alive—that's fine, but calling them anti-choice is just inaccurate and manipulative. Second, I really object to calling unborn children 'clumps of cells' or 'biologic product.' Those aren't even scientific terms. That 'clump of cells' has a unique DNA code from the very first moments of conception. It is always human, and it is always a human individual. Whether you think it's alive or a 'person' is another matter, but it's just deceitful to describe a fetus as a 'clump of cells.' A tumor is a clump of cells. A fetus is, unquestionably, human life."

As I spoke, the professor's eyes flashed in anger. Several students began hissing at the first words that came out of my mouth. I had to finish my comments at a near-shout, just so they could be heard over the outraged cries. When I finished, several students began yelling at me—accusing me of bigotry and disparaging my intelligence. The tirade continued, unabated, for several minutes. Throughout the verbal attack, the teacher stood to the side, arms folded, and glared at me. Although I'd been booed and hissed several times in that class and others, I was a bit shaken by the ferocity of the attack. My heart was pounding. I felt angry and wracked with self-doubt. Should I have spoken up? Are those points even worth making?

After class, I was approached by a small group of students. They were some of the more quiet members of the class. In fact, I did not recall one ever making a public comment. A woman spoke first. "Well, David. I thought you should know that some of us are beginning to change our minds about abortion."

"Really?" I was amazed at the comment.

"Yeah, but don't get cocky. It was nothing you said. It was the reaction you got. If their position is correct, why do they feel the need to drown you out—to attack you personally? If they can't argue rationally, then they must be hiding something." Several of the group nodded in agreement.

I was moved by the support and thanked God for providing me with some evidence that my public comments were, perhaps, almost worth the abuse. However, I was also discouraged by the student's last statement to me as she and her friends walked away: "Don't tell anyone I told you this." She said it with a smile, but I could tell that she was serious. She did not want to endure what I had endured, and I could not blame her.

Some readers will laugh at the "intimidation" that I report. They will see my stories as nothing but the self-pitying, self-promoting whining of an obnoxious lawyer. Others will think that I am, once again, doing nothing more than universalizing personal experience. Even if my reports are true, they prove nothing.

However, I believe that my experience is an accurate expression of academic realities. In fact, my experience with intimidation is insignificant compared with the intimidation experienced by Christian and conservative students around the nation. Think of TCF. The senior leaders were confronted with graffiti, daily mockery, sit-ins, and physically intimidating "silent" protesters. Consider other examples:

- At the University of Wisconsin, campus activists besieged the offices of the student newspaper and stole virtually its entire stock of papers for having the audacity to print David Horowitz's paid advertisement that presented arguments against reparations for slavery.[3]
- At the University of Pennsylvania, Cornell University, and Dartmouth, campus activists stole and sometimes burned conservative student newspapers—without facing any significant penalty from the administration.
- At Cornell University a tenured professor faced sexual discrimination complaints and found his job in jeopardy after he posted on his office bulletin board material that opposed a local gay rights ordinance.

- At Harvard Law School a Federalist Society member who wrote an article opposing gay rights legislation found his face pasted over graphic gay pornography and posted throughout the school. The administration made no effort to punish the wrongdoers.
- Georgetown University's student newspaper fired a conservative columnist for angering campus feminists with his weekly columns.

These examples are just one ridge of a mountain of intimidation. In *The Shadow University*, Alan Charles Kors and Harvey L. Silverglate provide hundreds of pages of examples of intimidation, coercion, and oppression on the modern campus.[4] Even a cursory review of conservative publications and news sites like *National Review, National Review Online, Townhall.com, CNSnews,* and the *Weekly Standard* reveals an almost monthly (and sometimes weekly) litany of collegiate outrages. Unless an evangelical student remains completely silent, he or she should expect not just persistent arguments against his position (reeducation) but also verbal and sometimes physical intimidation.

Exclusion

The gospel, however, is difficult to silence. In spite of the reeducation and in spite of the intimidation, Christians still flourish on secular campuses. When I arrived at Harvard Law School, the law school's Christian Fellowship was a struggling band of less than twenty students. By the time I left, the group had more than doubled in size. We had helped organize an apologetics seminar, entitled the Veritas Project, that was attended by more than a thousand members of the Harvard community. We watched classmates accept Christ, and we praised God as we became one of the largest, most active, most ethnically diverse student groups on campus. Our Friday night praise and worship services would last for hours, and the week was filled with prayer meetings, Bible studies, and book discussion groups. To this day my Christian Fellowship comrades are my closest and dearest friends. It is their prayers that I value the most, their counsel that I seek when in need.

The Harvard Law School Christian Fellowship is hardly unique. When I taught at Cornell Law School, I had the honor to speak to several of the undergraduate Christian fellowships. I spoke to Cornell Christian Fellowship, Grace Christian Fellowship, and the Chinese Bible Study. Each of these groups counted almost one hundred members. Campus Crusade for Christ was a large and powerful presence. These large Christian organizations were supported and complemented by legions of smaller groups like Alpha Chi, Japanese Bible Study, the Christian Legal Society, the Singaporan Bible Study, and the Graduate Christian Fellowship.

Although Christians still constituted a small minority of the thousands of Cornell undergraduates; graduate, and professional school students; faculty; and staff, the Christian presence was unmistakable. At times, advertisements for Christian meetings were so prevalent, I felt like I'd returned to Lipscomb.

The Tufts Christian Fellowship, before it was banned from campus, was arguably the university's largest and most active student organization. Other Christian fellowships that I have spoken to or represented are often large and usually growing. Student-led Christian groups—so obvious in high schools—are becoming prominent members of the campus community. So long as Christians can speak, the gospel flourishes.

When reeducation and intimidation fail, campus activists are left with but one option: exclusion. The Tufts experience is indicative. There student activists (and many administrators and faculty members) were not content with relentless arguments against TCF's position, nor were they even satisfied by intimidation. They wanted TCF banished, and they would allow no force of law or fairness to deter them from their goal. They pushed the Judiciary into ignoring campus procedures and into holding a secretive midnight meeting. Without bothering to give TCF notice or an opportunity to be heard, the Judiciary ejected TCF from campus. A suspected terrorist before a military tribunal would have a greater opportunity to defend himself than the Tufts Judiciary initially gave the Tufts Christian Fellowship. However, to the radical campus left, TCF was a malignant tumor that had to be excised—immediately.

While the coercion and intimidation of campus conservatives and evangelicals is a long-standing and well-documented phenomenon, the recent wave of campus student groups banned or facing banishment on the basis of alleged "discrimination" is a relatively new development. When I first began working with InterVarsity Christian Fellowship as chief counsel for their Religious Freedom Crisis Team, InterVarsity officials told me that, in their experience, InterVarsity groups faced administrative threats "about once, perhaps twice, per year." While even one threat is alarming, given InterVarsity's size and reach—more than 34,000 students and faculty at 560 campuses—these periodic problems hardly represented a crisis.

By the year 2000, things had changed. In that year alone I represented or advised InterVarsity chapters at Tufts, the University of North Florida, Purdue University, Grinnell College in Iowa, and Middlebury College and Castleton State College in Vermont. In addition, I knew of problems with InterVarsity chapters at Williams College in Massachusetts and Whitman College in Washington. Additionally, non-InterVarsity Christian fellowships at Ball State in Indiana and the State University of New York (SUNY) in Oswego faced threats or outright bans.

That is ten colleges or universities in one academic year. What began as a nuisance is beginning to emerge as a trend. And for each embattled fellowship, the issue was the same: alleged violation of campus antidiscrimination regulations. Christian organizations that use the Bible as a guide for decision making find that they simply cannot operate without violating expansive nondiscrimination policies. With sexual orientation added to the nondiscrimination mix, Christians are becoming increasingly vulnerable. At some schools (Middlebury and Tufts), problems arose when openly gay students asked to be considered for leadership positions. At others (Purdue, Castleton, and SUNY), the fellowships found their existence imperiled when administrations began enforcing policies that required all student organizations to draft group constitutions that contained pledges not to discriminate on the basis of sexual orientation—the liberal version of a loyalty oath.

Liberals who require this nondiscrimination loyalty oath do so while loudly claiming to protect freedom. What they are protecting is the "freedom" of gay individuals to belong to (and lead) any group that they desire. The freedom that they do not support (and sometimes do not even acknowledge) is the freedom of expressive association—the freedom to sometimes exclude.

What makes this argument dangerous is its fundamental emotional power. Americans—even most conservative or evangelical Americans—tend to abhor discrimination. Everyone should be given an opportunity to succeed, and no one should be barred from success simply because of skin color, gender, disability, religion, and now sexual orientation. Antidiscrimination statutes that are designed, for example, to keep a law firm from firing a man just because he's a Jew or a restaurant from serving a woman simply because she's black, are powerful instruments of public validation. If a group is protected by an antidiscrimination regulation, then society is telling that group either (a) you have unjustly suffered over the years, and it is time to stop that suffering; or (b) there is nothing wrong with your status/ identity, and we will use the force of law to keep your identity from hindering you in anything you want to do.

Sometimes, both (a) and (b) apply. For African-Americans antidiscrimination statutes serve as both a redress for past wrongs and a powerful symbol of present acceptance. With respect to antidiscrimination rules that protect from discrimination on the basis of religion, (a) is much less true than (b). America has long been (relative to other countries) religiously tolerant. So, religious protections do not redress past wrongs so much as they enshrine that ethic of tolerance.

Although many gay rights activists insist that they deserve protection—like African-Americans—because of reasons (a) and (b), their argument is ultimately unsustainable. By most measures, gay individuals are just as educated and prosperous as the population at large. Though they have undeniably faced hatred and sometimes even violence, as a group, they are no worse off socially and economically than the rest of the population. Consequently, for the gay man or the lesbian, antidiscrimination statutes are not so much an engine of economic advancement as they are a symbol of public validation. Just as we protect religious people from discrimination because we value America's religious heritage and traditions of religious tolerance, they proport that we should protect gay individuals from discrimination because we value their unique culture and identity.

However, the longer the list of protected groups becomes, the greater the possibility that those protections will conflict with each other and with cherished, fundamental freedoms. In my discussion of the Tufts situation, I called the battle between TCF's religious freedoms and Tufts' antidiscrimination policies "the irresistible force against the immovable object." If you ask most Americans if they support religious freedom, freedom of speech, and freedom of association, they will emphatically answer yes. If you ask those same people if they support antidiscrimination statutes, including statutes that explicitly protect gays, then they will also answer yes. However, you simply cannot support both equally. One value must trump the other. How, for example, could the Tufts Judiciary protect religious freedom without, in some way, limiting the options of gay students? How can gay students be given unlimited options without, in some way, limiting the religious freedom of conservative religious students?

The most prominent public example of the conflict between the First Amendment and antidiscrimination is the Supreme Court's recent decision in *Boy Scouts of America v. Dale*.[5] As you probably recall from media reports, that case involved a gay former Eagle Scout's attempt to challenge the Boy Scouts' ban on gay scoutmasters. James Dale, the gay scout, argued that antidiscrimination provisions of New Jersey state law compelled the Boy Scouts to change their policy. The Supreme Court, in a bitterly contested 5-4 decision, disagreed, holding that the Boy Scouts' First Amendment rights to free speech and free association protected them from the reach of the government's antidiscrimination rules. The Court explained: "While the law is free to promote all sorts of conduct in place of harmful behavior, it is not free to interfere with speech for no better reason than promoting an approved message or discouraging a disfavored one, however enlightened either purpose may strike the government."

The importance of the *Boy Scouts* decision cannot be overstated. The government—whether represented by a mayor, a state agency, a public high school, or a public university—simply cannot use its antidiscrimination policies to dictate the leadership or membership criteria of religious or other expressive organizations.

It is safe to say, however, that the *Boy Scouts* decision is almost universally reviled on the modern, liberal campus. When the president of SUNY Oswego's Christian Fellowship brought the Supreme Court's ruling to the attention of a campus official that had banned the group from campus, she replied that she was not bound by "homophobic" legal pronouncements. The administration relented but only after intervention from the American Center for Law and Justice.

When Purdue University sought to require new student organizations to agree not to discriminate on the basis of sexual orientation, the administration backed down only after I wrote a letter that comprehensively explained the holding and implications of the *Boy Scouts* decision. Purdue, however, did not go quietly. A university vice president called the associate dean of the Law School and complained to him that I had written my letter on Cornell letterhead (a common practice when university teachers do consulting work) and pressured him to take action against me. Thankfully, the associate dean laughingly interpreted the call as an attempt to "rattle my cage."

While public universities are compelled, reluctantly, to comply with the Supreme Court's pronouncements, private universities are free to ignore the *Boy Scouts* decision—and often do. As I discussed earlier in the book, the Constitution only protects individuals and organizations from the government, not from private organizations.

There are good reasons for this seeming injustice. Private colleges need protection from governmental interference every bit as much as other private organizations (like Christian fellowships) need protection. If private colleges did not enjoy the full panoply of constitutional freedoms, then Christian colleges could not exist. In a free country, individuals and groups are permitted to form schools that serve only Christians, or only Jews, or only gays. Students who don't like the polices of a private school are, of course, free not to attend.

However, a large proportion of our nation's universities are private schools that do not exist for the primary purpose of advancing a particular religious viewpoint. These secular, religiously neutral schools, while not exactly welcoming Christians with open arms, have not traditionally opposed a Christian presence.

That changing reality is the point of this section. Private, secular colleges are increasingly reaching the conclusion that while their students may have a range of freedoms, they most definitely do not have the freedom to discriminate. These private colleges—colleges such as Harvard, Yale, Tufts, Dartmouth, and many other prominent educational institutions—are free to take decisive actions against Christian organizations and individuals, actions that would be plainly illegal if undertaken by a public university. For Christians at many of those schools (an increasing number), the sad reality is that they are no longer welcome on campus.

During my brief tenure at Cornell Law School, I had the honor of serving on the school's admissions committee. Although my colleagues on the committee were uniformly liberal—some radically so—I liked and respected virtually all of them. I consider them friends.

It was the committee's job to decide the "tough" admission. We made affirmative action decisions and discussed admissions files that were unique in some way. In short, whenever the dean of admissions had a concern, he brought the case to the committee.

One afternoon, we reviewed a particularly interesting file. The student had graduated near the top of his class from a small college, and he was in the process of finishing up a graduate program. His law school admissions test scores were in the top second or third percentile, and he was active with a variety of civic and political organizations. Although he was a white male (a definite handicap in law school admissions), he was such an accomplished student that his admission would ordinarily be routine. Why were we reviewing this file?

The reason was all too obvious. This applicant had graduated from a conservative Christian college, and he was attending a conservative Christian seminary. His civic activities included a stint pastoring a church, and his political involvement included a year spent working on the ill-fated presidential campaign of a noted Christian conservative.

One of the committee members questioned whether the school needed his obvious "Bible-thumping." Another noted that his "God-squadding" would not be welcome in the student community.

I spoke up. I told the committee that my background was "so religious that it makes this guy look like a heathen, and I did just fine in law school." Everyone laughed, and the candidate was admitted. After the meeting, one of the professors came to me and apologized for his comments. He had not meant to offend me or to appear antireligious.

I accepted his apology and bear no hard feelings toward him or anyone else on the committee. However, I was saddened at how even the most well-meaning, kindest liberals I've ever met had an immediate and strong reaction against a candidate that was so transparently Christian. The first impulse of more than one committee member was, obviously, to exclude him—to deny him admission to an Ivy League school and to all of the privileges and advantages that flow from a Cornell education. I thought back to my own law school application. I began my personal essay with a simple statement: "I am a Christian." Three years after graduation, I obtained a copy of my application from the Harvard admissions office. (I had to provide a copy to the Kentucky Bar Association as part of my bar application.) When I looked at the application, I was struck by the fact that the words *Christian* or *Christ* were circled or underlined every place they appeared. When I first saw that, I thought nothing of it. But now, I wonder, was there a similar debate about me? How many Christians have faced similar challenges when there was no one to advocate for them? How many have been excluded?

Given the seemingly relentless tide of reeducation, intimidation, and exclusion described in the preceeding pages, Christians could be excused for despairing at our prospects for impacting the secular university. However, even within the vast wasteland of political correctness lie seeds of hope. The church of the left's own power and arrogance have given Christians an opportunity to become voices of reason and freedom. The conclusion of TCF's story illustrates both the challenges to and the hopes of Christians in the secular academy.

6

Hearings and Hopes

A Blueprint for Transforming the College Campus

During the summer of 2000, media interest in TCF's plight subsided, but my work did not. Virtually every week, I was on the telephone with Tufts' counsel, trying to see if we could reach an agreement that would avoid the necessity of a hearing. The previous semester's media struggle had left its mark at Tufts. Initially, I thought we had made our points, that we had succeeded in persuading Tufts that religious freedom and freedom of association were preferable to ideological tyranny. I hoped that we had reached a turning point.

I was wrong. Although TCF never offered to surrender its religious freedom, it did offer significant concessions to Tufts. We offered to surrender all student activity fee funding, and we offered to make constitutional changes that would make TCF's leadership selection process more transparent. Tufts, however, was not able to make a decision. Our arguments and the resulting media attention had only served to galvanize our opposition. A significant minority of Tufts' decision makers not only wanted a hearing to happen, they wanted to see TCF destroyed.

Other, more moderate Tufts officials viewed a possible public hearing as a "teachable moment." In other words, the administration would abdicate its responsibility for creating a truly diverse educational environment and instead delegate critical educational decisions to students, hoping that the "process" would be educational. To TCF, the prospect of enduring more "process" was almost unbearable.

My negotiations were given urgency by the fact that my great friends and fellow warriors, Curtis and Jody Chang, had left Tufts. Curtis was on sabbatical, putting the finishing touches on a new book, and they had relocated to Oakland, California. I felt their loss deeply. Curtis had contacts in the administration and in the local and national media that had been invaluable, and Jody's day-to-day presence with TCF had helped spiritually stabilize a group that was attacked from all sides. In their absence, the on-site burden of responding to media inquiries and campus attacks fell to the TCF students themselves, specifically the new senior leaders. I did not look forward to fighting a new battle without Curtis and Jody.

By early August I began to see a hearing as inevitable. Tufts' counsel warned me that campus activists were pressing for a hearing as soon as possible, and there was no way that the wheels of academic bureaucracy would move fast enough to enact new policies that would guarantee TCF's existence. By the middle of the month, I forgot entirely about negotiation and focused all my efforts on preparing the TCF senior leaders for the coming ordeal.

Legally, I was more prepared for this hearing than for any hearing in my career. Not only had I read every word of the various Tufts handbooks; I had thoroughly researched every nuance of Massachusetts and federal law. InterVarsity Christian Fellowship had hired me to write a religious freedom handbook for their staff workers, and I had spent countless hours studying the religious rights of college students and student groups. By the beginning of the fall semester, I could fairly be called an expert in student religious freedom.

What I discovered, at least with respect to Tufts, was depressing. As I mentioned earlier, because Tufts was a private school, the Constitution was of no help to TCF. Not even the Supreme Court's recent decision in *Boy Scouts of America v. Dale* meant anything to us. Had Tufts been a public university, the *Boy Scouts* decision would have ended our case. The government would have been barred from forcing a Christian organization to open leadership positions to individuals who disagreed with the group's religious philosophies. The group's First Amendment rights would have trumped the government's nondiscrimination rules.

However, Tufts was not the government, and it had the freedom—if Tufts chose to exercise it—to ban every Christian organization and even every Christian from campus. TCF had no First Amendment rights at Tufts. TCF had only those rights that Tufts gave it, and those rights were extremely limited. In short, we had a right to exist only if we did not violate the Tufts nondiscrimination policy. We had to prove to the Judiciary that our decision to deny Julie Catalano a leadership position was not based on her sexual orientation.

If we lost before the Judiciary, then our options were extremely limited. Unlike the formal legal system, which allows litigants to appeal virtually every aspect of a lower court's decision, the Tufts judicial system only allowed appeals based on denials of "fair process." In other words, as long as the Judiciary did everything correctly during the hearing—such as providing TCF with notice, enough time to present its case, the opportunity to have an advocate present, and the opportunity to question witnesses—then its decision could not be reconsidered. We had one opportunity for survival.

When we looked at the panel, we were not optimistic about our chances. Most of the Judiciary's seven members were holdovers from the previous year—from the group that had already voted TCF off campus once. One of the new members had run for office on an anti-TCF platform. Another member was Julie Catalano's former roommate. Several TCF members thought our case was hopeless. They had high hopes that we would be able to reach a negotiated solution over the summer, and when that did not happen, despair set in.

But the despair was only temporary. God was at work. He first gave us clarity of thought as we prepared for the case. We distilled all of our potential arguments into a simple, coherent statement: We had not discriminated on the basis of sexual orientation; we had discriminated instead on the basis of sexual practice and religious belief. Although we had known Julie Catalano's sexual orientation for years, we did not take action until she stated an intention to change her sexual practice and declared a change in her religious beliefs.

We even began to work kernels of the gospel message into our legal argument. We all have sinful "orientations," whether they be toward homosexual sex, adulterous heterosexual sex, pride, greed, and such, but the beauty of the gospel is that Christ's blood transforms us all. We all have access to His grace, and we all must attempt to observe His commands. There are many "orientations," we argued, but there is only one standard.

TCF's response to Julie exemplified the gospel message. When she first disclosed her sexual orientation, she was not shunned, nor was she judged. Instead, they greeted her as a fellow sister in Christ. Close friendships flowered, and she was viewed as a leader in the group. Things changed only when she rejected biblical standards. The relevant issue was belief, not orientation.

As God gave us an argument, He also raised up a new generation of courageous servants. To this day I am deeply impacted by the courage, the wisdom, and the love of the TCF senior leaders. Tufts' policies limited a student group's advocate to a ten-minute closing argument, so the lion's share of the presentation would have to be made by the senior leaders themselves. They had to represent Christ to the Judiciary and to the Tufts community. The most critical aspects of the most critical student religious freedom case in the country fell to these four seniors.

I look back on my own college experience and wonder how I would have handled the challenge. For me, college was a fun experience. I took on a few challenges, but I was primarily interested in dating, spending time with friends, and planning my future. For the TCF senior leadership, their senior year would be very different. They would be the focus of campus hatred and ridicule. They would walk to class over sidewalks covered in anti-Christian graffiti. They would open the student newspaper to see their faith reviled in editorial after editorial. They would be in the epicenter of America's culture war.

Opening Salvos

Almost immediately after school started, the first shots were fired at TCF. To "educate" the Tufts community on the upcoming hearing, a coalition of student groups began handing out "fact sheets" to students. These "fact sheets" described how TCF pushed Julie Catalano to the brink of suicide, how InterVarsity Christian Fellowship advocated "reparative therapy," a practice allegedly condemned by the American Psychological Association, and how TCF was now directly attacking Tufts' commitment to diversity and tolerance.

The "fact sheet" was followed by editorials (called "Viewpoints" in Tufts vernacular) in the campus paper and by persistent graffiti on campus sidewalks. TCF was labeled "unsafe," "homophobic," and "bigoted." TCF senior leaders responded with Viewpoints of their own, but they were washed away by a tidal wave of hate speech.

The media glare—white-hot in May—had fizzled to only sporadic inquiries by September. Without Curtis and Jody, we felt that we did not have the resources to mount another media blitz, and we worried that more media attention might harden hearts on campus. Already there was a real sense on campus that "outsiders" (conservative outsiders) were forcing Tufts to back away from its commitment to "tolerance" and "diversity." TCF made the difficult decision to pull away from its media allies and concentrate its efforts on winning hearts and minds on the campus itself.

The hearing was set for Friday, 13 October 2000. By the first week in October, the tension on campus was almost unbearable. Although the senior leaders were performing magnificently, they were outnumbered. Tufts' administrators appeared to be siding with the gay activists, and student opinion itself seemed to harden against TCF. Activists were hammering at the idea that TCF was not just discriminatory, but also "unsafe"—too dangerous for the campus. TCF's early admonition to Julie that she should pray about her sexual orientation was twisted into an endorsement of reparative therapy. To gay activists, reparative therapy—the practice of counseling homosexual individuals to change their sexual orientation—fosters self-hatred and results in despair and suicide. Most members of TCF had barely even heard of reparative therapy, and InterVarsity has never endorsed the practice. No matter. To campus activists TCF's prayer requests were little better than electroshock therapy.

On Wednesday, 11 October, I drove to Tufts. For most of the five-hour drive from Ithaca to Boston, I prayed. I asked God to give me wisdom and courage, and I asked the Holy Spirit to speak through the senior leaders. I also prayed for patience. I knew the other side would use lies, intimidation, and inflated rhetoric, and my fury at their dishonesty could easily harden my heart. I prayed for Julie Catalano and her supporters, and I prayed that they would not see any trace of bigotry in our hearts or hear any bigotry in our words. Regardless of the outcome, I wanted the hearing to be a showcase for the love of Christ.

I was not the only one praying. When I arrived at Tufts, I found the most dynamic, committed group of college Christians I had ever seen. As soon as I arrived, we prayed, and we kept praying throughout our preparations. We were all of one heart and mind. We wanted to win the case, but, more than that, we wanted to uphold the name of Christ. We knew that the Judiciary and many others at the the hearing would have a stereotyped view of Christians as dangerous, hate-filled bigots. They expected the Klan. We would give them Christ.

The Hearing

The hearing was scheduled to begin at 5:00 P.M. in a conference room at Tufts' student center. We arrived at the student center about five minutes early and were greeted with a chilling scene. Campus activists had vowed to hold a candlelight vigil outside the hearing room, and they had turned out in force. The halls were deliberately darkened, so the sensation on entering the building was not unlike that of entering a cave—a cave full of hate. TCF had decided to avoid direct confrontation and not send its members to the student center. Instead, they stayed at the InterVarsity house and vowed to keep praying until we returned. So only six of us—the four senior leaders, one former senior leader, and I—faced the angry crowd.

We walked through the vigil, past the glares and muttered comments of the protesters, and tried to enter the hearing room. The Judiciary quickly ushered us out, saying they had some preliminary matters to discuss. We spent the next forty minutes in those dark halls, waiting, while the Judiciary discussed procedure. Julie, her family, her witnesses, and her advocate hovered nearby. Occasionally, a protester would walk up to a senior leader, look him or her in the eyes, and stare, silently. Within minutes, at least one of the senior leaders was visibly shaking. Two others huddled in a corner and began praying. I stood by myself, thought about our case, and marveled at the surreal scene before me.

This is it, I thought. *This is American higher education in the twenty-first century—Christians huddled in the corners of darkened halls, fighting for their very right to exist in the midst of a community that hates them.* I looked into the eyes of the protesters and did not see even a flicker of tolerance. I did not see a hint of interest in diversity. Instead, I saw only contempt. They were not there to engage us in dialogue, and they were certainly not there to experience a "teachable moment"; they had come to expel the infidels, to cleanse the impurity from their holy place.

When we finally entered the hearing room, I realized the playing field was even more unbalanced than I imagined. Under university rules, if a hearing was closed—and Julie had requested that it be closed—then no one was allowed in the hearing room except the parties to the dispute, the parties' designated advocates, family, and witnesses. Our crew numbered six. More than a dozen individuals marched in behind Julie. She was accompanied by her mother and father, by her advocate, by the Director of Tufts' Center for Gay Lesbian Transgendered Bisexual Affairs, by at least one faculty member, by a liberal theologian, and by representatives from several of Tufts' minority student organizations.

These additional people were not witnesses to any of the conversations between Julie and TCF or to any events relevant to Julie's complaint. They were advocates, and they had come to make speeches on Julie's behalf. We had one advocate, and I was limited to a ten-minute closing argument. Julie had a half-dozen, and they intended to speak for hours.

Things soon went from bad to worse. Our first step was formally to request that Julie's former roommate step down from the Judiciary and recuse himself from hearing this case. He refused, stating that his friendship with Julie would play no part in his thinking on the case. We asked the Judiciary to vote him off the panel. They refused, and I could see that our request visibly angered some panelists.

The hearing rules called for a complex series of presentations. First, Julie would give her opening statement. After her statement, we would be given an opportunity to respond. Then the parties would question each other. Following the party questioning, witnesses would speak and be questioned, the parties would have one more opportunity to question each other, and, finally, the advocates would make ten-minute closing arguments. The chairperson of the Judiciary announced that she wanted the entire hearing to be limited to two hours. I took one look at Julie's glaring lineup of witnesses and laughed. Their testimony alone would take two hours.

Julie spoke first. She remained seated throughout her presentation and spoke with a controlled rage. She accused Jody Chang of trying to coerce her into reparative therapy, and she accused TCF of teaching her self-hatred. She told the Judiciary that she almost committed suicide because of TCF's failure to accept her sexual orientation, and she told that Judiciary that she was treated differently from anyone else at TCF because of her sexual orientation. She cast Jody as the equivalent of a cult leader, someone who used her age and relative spiritual experience to dominate and control the student members of TCF. Her presentation was eloquent, and it was powerful. However, large segments of it were not true.

Jody Chang had not tried to force Julie into reparative therapy. Instead, she had asked her simply to pray about her sexuality and had given her an InterVarsity Press book detailing an evangelical Christian view of sexual orientation. Far from placing unrelenting pressure on

Julie, Jody had rarely spoken about the issue with Julie, and conversations became intense only after Julie demanded that her new religious beliefs not be considered by TCF when she applied to be a senior leader. Moreover, Jody Chang was not a cult leader. She did not dominate and control TCF. Although Jody was certainly (and rightfully) respected by TCF's members and student leaders, she did not manipulate them. The senior leaders of TCF were independent, opinionated individuals who came to the decision to deny Julie's leadership application in their own ways. No one from TCF considered themselves under Jody Chang's control.

Additionally, Julie left several key factors out of her presentation. At the same time that TCF was allegedly pushing her toward suicide with its intolerance, she endured several personal crises that were completely unrelated to TCF or to her sexuality. It struck me as incredible that TCF was the sole cause for her despair.

At any rate, Julie's presentation placed us in a difficult position. We all knew that several of her key statements were false, and we were offended and hurt by the anger of her presentation. However, we also knew that we were not—no matter what happened—going to attack Julie Catalano. The senior leaders were adamant on that point. We would defend TCF's freedom, but we would not attack Julie.

The Judiciary turned to us, faces set. Our primary spokesperson, Jonathon, stood up and began to speak. His voice was quiet but firm. He first turned to Julie and declared that TCF would not attack her, and they harbored no bitterness against her. In fact, he said, TCF's leaders and members loved her and mourned her lost friendship. Julie stared back at him. Her face was locked in a scowl, but for the first time, her eyes began to moisten.

Jon then turned his attention back to the Judiciary. His message was simple. TCF did not discriminate against Julie on the basis of her sexual orientation. Far from it, we elevated her to leadership positions even after we knew that she considered herself lesbian or bisexual. It was only when she declared that her religious beliefs regarding sexuality and sexual practice changed that TCF was forced to take action. Her orientation was not the issue. Her beliefs were.

The Judiciary was not convinced. Jon was repeatedly interrupted and challenged. Julie asked aggressive questions, and many of Jon's responses were greeted with audible groans and visible disgust. They did not seem to believe a word he said. His compassion and conviction were thrown right back into his face.

At the height of the grilling, another senior leader, Nicole, began to speak. Nicole is a tenderhearted soul who used to count Julie as one of her closest friends. She could barely speak through her tears. She began with an apology. She looked directly at Julie and told her that she was sorry that Julie was so hurt, and she was sorry that she never knew. Nicole told Julie that if she had known Julie was suicidal, there was nothing she would not have done for her. Nicole told Julie that she missed their friendship and her presence in the Fellowship.

With tears still in her eyes, Nicole turned back to the Judiciary. Speaking calmly, but with emotion-laden words, she repeated much of what Jon had said, emphasizing again that it was not Julie's sexual orientation that had caused TCF's action. This time the Judiciary did not attack. I even noticed some of their expressions softening. *This is not going how they expected,* I thought. *They expected viciousness, and they expected hate. They're confused.*

After Nicole spoke, it was time for Julie's witnesses. I was ready for this moment. A tall black woman stood and began to speak. She gave her name and introduced herself as the president of the Pan-African Alliance. I was not permitted to speak, so I nudged Jon. He stood and objected.

The Judiciary seemed startled. The chairperson leaned forward. "Why are you objecting?"

"These people aren't witnesses. They're advocates. They don't know anything about this case. They don't have actual knowledge of the events of this case, which is how the rule book defines a witness. They're just here to make arguments. That's the role of an advocate."

"Is this true?" the chair asked Julie. "Do they know anything about this case?"

Julie sprang up. "Before this hearing, I asked the dean of students who I could bring as witnesses, and he told me that I could bring representatives of different student groups to talk about the antidiscrimination policy—to discuss why you should enforce the policy."

Gotcha! I was madly scribbling notes to Jon. "You talked to the dean of students?" Jon asked. I turned to the back of the room and stared at the dean. He was sitting beside the university's lawyer, looking like he wanted to hide under a desk. "Dean Reitman, is this true?" Jon confronted the dean directly.

"Dean Reitman, what did you tell Julie?" The chairperson wanted answers as well.

"I told her that she could have individuals come and speak about their experience and perceptions regarding the antidiscrimination policy. I guess it really depends upon what 'witness' means . . ."

I did not even have to listen to the rest. The dean's decision to allow Julie to bring these additional witnesses into the hearing was improper, and the Judiciary knew it. Several of the members of the Judiciary had spent months being excoriated by the press for the unfairness of last semester's midnight meeting, and they were determined to do everything correctly in this hearing. Now, the dean of students had just handed us a perfect ground for appeal. The Judiciary turned to Julie, looking for a way out.

Julie did not back down, and neither did her witnesses. She wanted them to speak, and they wanted to speak. Several of them had brought prepared speeches. They were indignant. The Judiciary was caught in the middle. The chair turned to us.

"Let them speak," I whispered to Jon.

"What?" He was confused. We had them on the ropes, and he wanted those witnesses excluded. But I had another idea.

"If we let them speak, I know exactly what we can say. Besides, they're looking terrible right now. If we let them talk, we'll look good by comparison."

Jon's eyes lit up. He understood. He addressed the Judiciary. "We still object to the dean's involvement, but we'll let them talk." He turned to Julie's first witness, the head of Tufts' Pan-African Alliance. "Go ahead."

The reaction from the Judiciary was immediate. "Thank you!" The chair was relieved. Then she addressed the witnesses. "You can speak, but understand that we don't have to consider your statements if we feel that they don't have any bearing on what happened between Julie and the TCF."

Visibly angered, Julie's first witness began speaking. She told the Judiciary that the antidiscrimination policy was critical and that the Pan-African Alliance took it so seriously that it had even voted to allow a white vice president to serve a largely black organization. Her group was tolerant. Ours was bigoted. It was that simple.

Before she could sit down, Jon raised his hand. "I just have one question for this witness."

"Go ahead."

"Would you ever vote for or allow a member of the Ku Klux Klan to lead the Pan-African Alliance?"

Her response was instantaneous. "No. We would not allow a bigot to run our group."

"So, you believe that your group should be allowed to select leaders who share the beliefs of the group?"

At that moment she realized what she had said, and so did the Judiciary. I felt like I could literally watch the lights go on over the heads of several of the panelists. One of them even looked at me and smiled. There was a moment of unspoken communication. *I understand you now. I understand exactly what you're saying.*

After the president of the Pan-African Alliance stepped down, the leader of Hillel, the university's largest Jewish student group, stood to speak. Her message was similar. She told the Judiciary that several non-Jews had held leadership positions with Hillel. Before she even finished her statement, one of the panelists confronted her. "Would you allow a Holocaust denier to hold a leadership position with Hillel?" She stammered and stuttered, trying to evade the question. The panelist cut her off. "I didn't think so."

The tide had turned. Each witness that followed was discredited by a single question, sometimes two. The Judiciary began to be visibly annoyed at the witnesses' strident tones, evasive answers, and irrelevant accusations. A dormitory resident assistant was dismissed after saying that he had seen anti-gay hate speech but never anti-Christian. "But what about the graffiti all over campus? That's all against Christians. What do you think about that?"

His response was incredible. "That speech isn't in the dorms. If you'll note, in my statement, I specifically said I hadn't seen anything anti-Christian in the dorms."

The Judiciary laughed. One of them spoke up. "That's ridiculous. You didn't answer the question. What do you think about all the anti-Christian graffiti?"

"That's people just expressing their opinion."

The Judiciary laughed again. I was amazed. This group of students, this "kangaroo court" was actually listening to reason. They were taking their duties seriously and trying to do the right thing. I was even more amazed when they refused even to look at documents Julie tried to submit that purported to show how Christians used the Bible to justify slavery. Their hearts were softening.

"Thank you, God." I prayed. "And forgive me for judging these kids."

I was not the only one who sensed the change. Julie's witnesses grew increasingly shrill, and, when it was time for our witness's testimony, I could tell that the other side was desperate.

Our principal witness, Ohene, was one of the senior leaders who had voted to deny Julie's leadership application. When he was at Tufts, he was one of the most popular students on campus and also a leader in the campus civil rights community. In fact, Ohene had even demonstrated in favor of policies that protected gays from workplace discrimination. Although he had graduated, he still knew several members of the Judiciary, and they knew him.

Ohene spoke for more than two hours. This entire dispute had wounded him to his core. More than anyone else, he had tried to find a way to allow Julie to lead without compromising TCF's principles and, when no way could be found, no one was more hurt. Several times he had reached out to Julie, begging her to moderate her stance, and she had refused. In the final analysis, when faced with a decision between friendship and what he believed to be God's will, he chose God.

By the time Ohene stepped down, the hearing had been going for almost seven hours. We were all exhausted. Ohene's testimony—so clear at the beginning—had been muddled by emotion and by intense questioning. Many members of the Judiciary had wept during portions of Ohene's testimony, and Julie herself had nearly been overcome with emotion. All of the testimony was finished. No more questions could be asked. It was time for the last act. It was time for closing arguments. Finally, I could speak.

I had two primary goals for my oral argument. The first was to summarize the evidence and present a coherent legal argument explaining how TCF had not violated the Tufts antidiscrimination policy. My second, and most important, goal was to try to convince the Judiciary that ruling for TCF was simply the right thing to do. I learned early in my legal career that it is not enough to argue that the law is on your side. You must also argue that your client deserves to win, that it would be unjust if your client lost.

I began by framing the issue in front of the Judiciary. "Julie Catalano has alleged that TCF discriminated against her on the basis of her sexual orientation. However, if you've been listening carefully, you'll note that she has not presented a shred of evidence that this is true." Several members of the Judiciary appeared skeptical. I pressed on. "We've proven that Julie first told TCF leaders about her sexual orientation when she was still a freshman. TCF knew that she considered herself lesbian or bisexual years ago, and despite this knowledge, they gave her several leadership positions. She led Bible studies and led TCF's women's accountability group."

Throughout my presentation I was aware that Julie's advocate and many of her witnesses were glaring at me and rolling their eyes at almost every word I said. I hoped that the Judiciary noticed that disrespect. "By her senior year she was a leading candidate to become a senior leader, but something changed—and it wasn't her sexual orientation. It was her religious beliefs. She no longer believed what the group believed, and she stated that she expected to engage in sexual practices that the group thought were wrong. So they decided that she should not be a leader. TCF didn't kick her out of the club. They just decided that she couldn't help run the group. It's that simple."

Julie's advocate began scribbling on his notepad. I continued talking, explaining in detail how TCF's actions did not violate Tufts' policies. I could feel the clock ticking. I was taking up too much time with technicalities. Time to switch to my closing thoughts—to the emotional heart of the argument.

"Tufts prides itself on being a diverse community, and it prides itself on welcoming students of all backgrounds. Tonight that commitment to diversity is put to the test. TCF is committed to diversity. It has never said that there shouldn't be a student organization committed to gay and lesbian issues. In fact, TCF is glad that Julie has found a home at Tufts. She's a leader of a different group—one that has different beliefs regarding homosexuality, and she is a member of TTLGBC (Tufts' Transgender Lesbian Gay Bisexual Collective). The other side, however, is against diversity. The other side says it wants people of all backgrounds at Tufts, but only as long as they believe what we want them to believe. They want Latino students at Tufts, but only as long as they're not serious about their Catholic heritage. They want Arab students at Tufts, but only as long as they're not actually Muslim. They want Jewish students, but no orthodox Jews, and they want black students, but only if they've abandoned much of the religious tradition and heritage of the black community.

"In other words, Tufts is saying that a religious tradition that spans the millennia, that provides comfort to hundreds of millions of people, is not welcome here. If you say that evangelical or conservative Christians are not welcome at Tufts, then you are rejecting more than just TCF. You are rejecting the likes of William Wilberforce, the man who—more than anyone else—was responsible for ending the slave trade. You are saying that Mother Theresa is not the kind of person we want at Tufts, and yes, you're even saying that you don't want the likes of Martin Luther King Jr.—a black Baptist who held many views that Tufts would find abhorrent.

"Julie Catalano has a home at Tufts University, and we're glad for that. These senior leaders," I pointed to the four students sitting around me, "are fighting for their home, their place in this community. Don't take that home away."

I took a deep breath and offered a silent prayer. *Please, God, let them hear my words.* I was still praying when Julie's advocate began his final comments. He began by indignantly stating that he was offended and appalled by much of what I said, that it represented thinking that was "unacceptable." For ten minutes he railed against TCF, accusing them of fostering self-hatred, of almost killing Julie. He argued that the Judiciary's decision would be a referendum on the antidiscrimination policy. To Julie's advocate, banning TCF was nothing less than a moral necessity—a statement that the community had to make. Bigotry would not be tolerated. His words were angry, and his tone was contemptuous.

I watched the Judiciary carefully through his presentation, and I could tell that some of the panel were visibly disturbed by his tone and by some of his statements. His anger and contempt provided a startling contrast to the gentle conviction of the senior leaders. Only one side was hate-filled. Only one side was bigoted.

After Julie's advocate finished his closing, you could feel the tension leave the room. The hearing was over. The chair of the Judiciary asked everyone to leave so that the panel could begin its deliberation. I thanked some of the Judiciary members for their patience and their apparent open-mindedness, and I told the dean of students that I hoped that the hearing had given him a new perspective on TCF. With that, we walked back into the hall, back into the midst of the protests. The hearing had lasted almost eight full hours, but the protesters were still out in force, still glaring at the senior leaders as they walked, exhausted, back to the InterVarsity house.

The Decision

I left Boston on Saturday morning, still unsure of the outcome. I felt good about our presentation, but I kept second-guessing my closing argument. Had I said too much? Too little? Had I adopted the correct tone? The senior leaders had worked so hard and poured so much of themselves into that evening that I hated the thought that my own mistakes or my own poor performance could hurt their cause.

The self-doubt persisted until Monday morning. I was in my office, preparing to teach my class, when the phone rang. It was Jon.

"The J's made its decision. I've got it right here."

I felt my heart in my throat. "Did we win?"

"I'm not sure." Jon sounded hesitant. Almost defeated. "Here's what they said. They voted unanimously that our policies do not violate Tufts' antidiscrimination rules, and they voted unanimously that TCF should exist on campus. They even called us 'valuable.'"

"But?" All the news was good. Why was Jon sounding so upset?

"But they also ruled that we discriminated against Julie. They put us on probation. They said that our policies were OK, but that we didn't apply them. They said we let Ohene be a senior leader when he had the same religious beliefs about homosexuality as Julie."

"That's ridiculous. Ohene never said that."

"I know. What can we do?"

Jon was concerned, but I was elated. "Nothing. We're not going to do a thing. We won. This is tremendous. The Judiciary has not only said that we have a right to exist on campus; they've also said that our policies aren't discriminatory. TCF is alive, and it keeps its religious freedom. As for this other stuff . . . I don't know whether they honestly misinterpreted Ohene's testimony or if they willfully distorted it, but it doesn't matter. They're obviously trying to soften the blow to the other side. They're trying to give them something. It's completely meaningless. If you have any doubt that we won, watch how the other side reacts."

Jon chuckled. "You should check out the Internet message boards. They're furious."

After the conversation I went to a Web site frequented by the Tufts activist community. The first message commenting on the Judiciary's decision was from one of the leaders of the campus gay community. It stated, simply: "We lost!!!!!" The next message called for action, and dozens of messages echoed the sentiment. In the minds of Tufts student activists, the Judiciary had endorsed bigotry and gutted the antidiscrimination policy. More than a hundred students gathered to protest the ruling.

In their fury several student leaders lashed out at TCF, openly mocking Christians and Christianity. Days later a band of protesters stormed the administration building, occupied several offices, and vowed not to leave until Tufts antidiscrimination policy was amended so that it encompassed "self-acceptance" of identity. In other words, they wanted the policy amended so that it was a violation of Tufts policy for a group or for a student to advocate or teach that homosexual practice was wrong or that sexual orientation could be changed. To the protesters, any call for repentance or prayer regarding homosexual behavior or desire caused gay individuals not to accept themselves and was therefore discriminatory.

But they had gone too far. The mass of student opinion swung against the protesters. In their hatred and in their repression, they had revealed themselves, and most students were repulsed. The president of Tufts issued a legally meaningless statement that he always thought the antidiscrimination policy encompassed "self-acceptance" of identity. The protesters declared victory and left the building, discredited.

By the spring semester TCF's place was no longer in doubt. TCF and TTLGBC had even made tentative steps at reconciliation, culminating in a symposium jointly sponsored by the two groups. An evangelical Christian and a gay activist spoke about their relationship—how friendships can form and exist even when worldviews differ dramatically.

In May 2001, four courageous students graduated from Tufts University. They graduated as senior leaders of Tufts Christian

Fellowship, one of the campus's largest and most vibrant student groups. In my mind they graduated as heroes. They had faced bigotry, hatred, and persecution and had responded with courage, conviction, and love. They had returned good for evil, and they had helped preserve the gospel message, not only on their own campus, but at campuses across America. The enemy had come in like a flood, and in those four students the Lord had raised up a standard against him.

Freedom and Honesty

Against the rising tide of campus reeducation, intimidation, and conclusion, we can offer the example of the leaders of the Tufts Christian Fellowship. It is imperative that Christians develop a coherent legal and political strategy for preserving our presence on America's secular campuses, and TCF has shown us the way. The key is advocating two values that are revered by Americans of virtually all religious and political stripes: freedom and honesty.

In the public high schools, there is just enough favorable public sentiment and there are just enough predominantly Christian communities to deceive us into thinking that we can put religion back into public education. Yet few Christians hold any illusions that we can somehow officially "Christianize" our secular universities. Instead, many Christians seem almost frighteningly unconcerned with the plight of Christians on secular campuses.

Throughout the Tufts conflict the vast majority of TCF's support came not from fellow Christians but from secular civil libertarians. Both *Christianity Today* and *The 700 Club* covered the story, and several Christian ministries expressed interest in the situation, but most of the real offers of help—the real offers to join us in the trenches—came from secular conservative and libertarian columnists and activists. The

Foundation for Individual Rights in Education expressed more genuine concern for TCF than any other organization. I even received a call from an (unnamed) Christian legal defense organization, urging TCF not to file suit against Tufts.

At first I was puzzled by this discrepancy. Why were Christians not fighting for their own? I think there are three reasons: fear, suspicion, and lack of concern. First, it is clear that other Christians at Tufts—and Christians at other secular universities—are silenced by fear. If another Christian fellowship spoke up to support TCF, it would only expose its own policies to review and quite possibly find itself under the same persecution. "Besides," these groups argue, "we're about spreading the gospel, not fighting the culture war." This argument ignores the fact that it was the gospel itself that was attacked at Tufts, and if the gospel message was banned from one prominent campus, then that would unquestionably embolden activists at other campuses. Isolated fellowships could be picked off, one by one, with the gospel light being slowly extinguished in campus after campus.

However, if Christians demonstrated solidarity and collective courage, the exclusionary movement could be stopped in its tracks. Currently, campus activists only have the political strength to make a realistic effort to ban Christian groups at a few campuses, but that strength will grow if it is not checked. There are tens of thousands of evangelicals in America's secular colleges, and those evangelicals should let it be known that they will draw a line in the sand for religious freedom—everyone's religious freedom. By publicly standing for freedom, we can transform our campus image from moralizers to liberators.

Too often, however, even fearless Christians are immobilized by suspicion. In the past seven years, I've represented several dozen Christian organizations, churches, and Christian individuals, and many of those cases involved egregious religious persecution. The battle over Trinity's Spirit Life Center and Tufts Christian Fellowship are just two of the more dramatic examples. In every significant case I've taken, I've sought political or legal support from other Christian organizations. Every time I have sought that support, one or more organizations have turned me down—not out of fear but because they suspect that the Christian organization must have done something wrong or it wouldn't be facing a legal challenge.

A surprising number of Christians are arrogant enough to believe that if only they had been in charge, the Christian group would never have been in trouble. Some even believe "favor" from relevant authorities is an unmistakable sign of favor from God and persecution indicates divine displeasure. One Christian told me, "Daniel lived in the most hostile environment imaginable, and look at him. He ended up virtually running Babylon." I was flabbergasted. "Yes," I responded, "but only *after* he'd been thrown in the lion's den!"

Modern evangelicals are a relatively prosperous bunch. Most of the individuals who will read this book have nice homes and good jobs or are perhaps happily attending Christian colleges. In your experience teachers have liked you, employers compliment you and your Christian beliefs have proven beneficial, not just spiritually, but also educationally, professionally, and emotionally. It is frankly difficult to imagine your Christianity getting you in any real trouble, particularly when much of your experience has indicated the opposite. Therefore, when you hear about persecuted Christians (especially in America), you automatically become suspicious. "They must be moralist screamers," you think, or perhaps disturbing zealots of some kind. If they were only more (loving, compassionate, prudent, flexible, savvy, etc.), then there would be no trouble. Baptists do not trust the wisdom of Pentecostals, Pentecostals distrust other Pentecostals, and Protestants distrust Catholics. Ridiculous. Do we really believe that legal precedents that crush the fundamentalists next door, or even the most emotional Pentecostal congregations, cannot be used against your "solid, respectable" church? It is possible to support freedom without supporting every line of doctrine, every action, of the particular persecuted church.

Finally, I have detected a lack of concern for secular campus Christians from those who believe that Christian students should attend Christian colleges, or at least believe that the existence of a comprehensive network of Christian institutions mitigates the reeducation, intimidation, and exclusion of the secular campus. In other words, Christians may not be welcome at Williams, but we are always welcome at Wheaton. In fact, the Christian legal defense organization that urged me not to file suit against Tufts did so because they feared that any legal precedent against a private school could negatively impact the freedom of our Christian schools.

I agree that the network of Christian colleges is an invaluable spiritual resource, but their existence should not lull us into a false sense of security. Not all Christians are called to Christian colleges, and not all Christians thrive at Christian colleges. My greatest spiritual growth came when I was part of an embattled minority at Harvard, not when I was surrounded by like-minded evangelicals at Lipscomb. Further, because of a relative lack of Christian graduate and professional schools, doctors, lawyers, engineers, and scientists of all stripes are often forced into the secular academy to complete their schooling. For these individuals the existence of a Christian educational network is of little relevance or comfort.

However, the existence of this Christian educational network does considerably complicate our response to the secular educational challenge. We do not necessarily turn to the law to open up private, secular schools to Christian influence. In fact, we positively need to protect the freedom of these private schools. My unnamed Christian legal critic was correct to fear legal precedents that impair the freedom of private colleges to define themselves and set their own rules. He just misunderstood the nature of the legal claim I intended to bring against Tufts. We intended to use *moral argument* to persuade them that Christians belonged at Tufts and *legal coercion* only to force them to abide by their own rules and to require them to deal honestly with the public.

A Strategy for Change

The evangelical Christian community should take a three-pronged approach to fostering campus religious freedom. First, we should take maximum advantage of the freedoms we do have. Public university Christians, thanks to recent Supreme Court rulings, have several basic freedoms. Public university Christians are entitled to equal access (with other expressive organizations) to campus facilities, equal access to university funding, and freedom from university interference in their Christian group's internal governance and interference. Thanks to the impressive efforts of Campus Crusade for Christ, InterVarsity, and countless other denominational and church groups, campus Christian groups are vibrant and growing. The very size and visibility of these groups often make them ripe for administrative attack, but public university Christians can preserve the power and vitality of their ministries by knowing their rights and asserting them.

Second, evangelicals on private, secular campuses should make powerful moral, and occasionally legal, arguments in favor of academic freedom. Academic freedom is a value that retains a powerful appeal in the secular academy. In fact, prior to the P.C. revolution that swept American campuses in the eighties and early nineties, many private schools prided themselves on being more free than public schools. Students had *greater* expressive and associational rights. Where public schools sought to ban subversive student groups, private universities sometimes encouraged their formation and provided resources that helped them flourish.

Unfortunately, as I have detailed in this book, things have changed. Although sexual freedom thrives at secular campuses, freedom of expression, freedom of religion, and free association are stifled. We need to argue vigorously and courageously that a university that truly values education, diversity, and tolerance should value those classic First Amendment freedoms even more than the government does. Otherwise, they risk becoming, in the words of Curtis Chang, "the Bob Jones of the left."

We also need to argue that true academic freedom means employing Christian faculty members. Even if the university protects the independence and freedom of its students, it often denies Christians or conservatives access to coveted faculty positions. Through ideological litmus tests, intimidation, and mockery, many (if not most) humanities departments of major secular universities have been completely cleansed of a Christian presence. Consequently, even if the student body is genuinely diverse, the faculty is often ideologically monolithic. Individual Christian graduate students should decide today that this shall not stand. They should commit themselves to kicking down the door of the modern secular academy. Apply for secular faculty positions, and if the university violates the law or its own policies by excluding you because of your religion or point of view, do not be afraid to take legal action. If academic freedom means anything, it means that Christians have equal access to even the most prestigious positions in the secular academy.

Third, if a private university decides—as it has a right to do—that it will not allow the Christian perspective, that it will not truly protect academic freedom, then we should force that university to be honest. If you read the promotional brochures of even the most totalitarian liberal colleges, they will trumpet their commitment to diversity and tolerance. They will extol their campus's "welcoming" atmosphere for people from "all backgrounds." These statements are false. While they may be committed to ethnic diversity, they are not committed to ideological or religious diversity. While they may welcome people from some backgrounds, they do not welcome people from all backgrounds. If a college has made a decision to exclude Christians, or Jews, or Muslims, then we must force that school to disclose that decision.

A complex layer of laws protects consumers from false or misleading advertising. We should creatively use those laws to require schools honestly to advertise themselves. No student who sought to attend David Lipscomb University would ever be deceived into thinking that it was anything but an evangelical Christian school. Lipscomb promotes itself as a Christian school, trumpets its required daily Bible classes, and makes no secret of its strict disciplinary rules. In fact, those rules are a selling point for many parents. If an openly gay student decided to attend Lipscomb, then he could not complain that he did not know that Lipscomb prohibited extramarital sex.

Contrast the prospective Lipscomb student with a prospective student at any number of secular private institutions. A Christian could read every word of their promotional materials without understanding that they may not be able to practice their religion, or speak honestly regarding critical moral issues, or freely associate with other Christians while on campus. Far from it, the prospective student would believe they were entering a freewheeling, tolerant atmosphere, where ideas are exchanged and differences welcome, even encouraged. Then they would arrive, open their mouth, and discover that they had been lied to. Speech codes would stifle classroom discussion, and expansive nondiscrimination policies would limit if not prohibit evangelical organizations.

Our response to these universities is simple: We respect your right to define yourself—just do so honestly. Currently, the law requires more honesty from the maker of a thousand-dollar refrigerator or from the seller of a five-thousand-dollar used car than it does from an admissions officer who's selling a $120,000 higher education.

One consequence of honesty will be more freedom. One of the reasons why Christian universities struggle to achieve high national rank is that they have decreased the available student and faculty talent pool by selecting only Christians. Fewer bright students and fewer scholars are available to learn and teach, so the institution has difficulty matching the intellectual environment of the best secular schools. Honest schools on the left will soon find they will face the same problem. While there are many intelligent and charismatic gay activists, feminist scholars, and literary deconstructionists, a faculty and student body drawn exclusively from that talent pool will face many of the same limitations faced by Christians schools. The church of the left will soon face an inescapable choice: theological purity or secular glory. Most schools will find the diminished rank and glory of the theologically pure existence too bitter a pill to swallow and reembrace academic freedom. Some schools would prefer purity, and that is their right. There would, however, be no casualties of their deception.

Unfortunately, Christians must shoulder much of the blame for the plight of campus evangelicals. The public high school Christian faces potential persecution because unbalanced legal structures give religiously zealous liberals opportunities not provided to evangelical Christians. By contrast, the secular university Christian faces an unbalanced playing field not so much because the legal structures are unbalanced but because the entire field has been seized by the left. We have stood by while those hostile to Christianity have taken over faculties, administrations, and student groups. That is not the law's fault; it is ours. However, through God's grace and the work of many courageous Christians, we still have a toehold on campuses. And thanks to the repression of our opponents, we have a unique opportunity: to make campus Christianity synonymous with freedom. Remember, in secular America, we want all views to be heard. We do not fear truly free expression, because we know that of all the myriad viewpoints only one is presented with the power of the Holy Spirit.

7

Working for a Living

How Your Christianity Can Get You Fired

Few days are more liberating, more exuberant, than graduation day. Graduation from law school was one of the most enjoyable, memorable days of my life. The weather was beautiful, my mother and father were there, and my grandmother traveled from Mississippi to Boston to see her grandson graduate from Harvard. When I shook hands with the dean and received my diploma, I felt a tremendous sense of relief, pride, and exhilaration.

The day ended with a cruise in Boston Harbor. A classmate had rented a yacht and invited several dozen of us to enjoy dinner on the water. The food was delicious, the weather was perfect, and downtown Boston was breathtakingly beautiful. Late in the evening I noticed that my normally vivacious grandmother was sitting quietly alone on the stern of the boat, looking back at the shining city lights. Concerned, I walked up behind her and asked if she was OK. She turned and looked at me with shining eyes. "Everything's perfect, David. Someone just needs to shoot me now, while I'm happy."

I laughed, relieved. For her, an almost eighty-year-old former teacher, a woman who got her start in a one-room schoolhouse in rural Mississippi, this was a pinnacle moment. She dedicated herself to teaching not only her students but also her children and her grandchildren. Some of my earliest memories are of sitting in her lap, reading history textbooks and talking about George Washington, Thomas Jefferson, and Benjamin Franklin. She instilled in me a love of learning that ultimately led me to Harvard. At that moment, she was looking back on life and considering a job well done.

For me, the sensation was very different. Yes, I was happy to graduate and thankful for past accomplishments, but I was looking ahead. I was looking forward to being liberated from my poverty-stricken student experience, and I was eager to escape the heavy-handed, politically correct environment of the law school. I was returning home to the South. The "real world" beckoned, and I was already enjoying my new-found freedom.

However, I found the world to be much less free than I ever imagined. Within five years of graduation, I had endured intimidating lectures from feminist law partners and job interviews during which the interviewer explicitly told me that she found my Christian background "troubling." I had a senior partner of a law firm attempt to destroy my reputation and career simply because I represented a Christian client against a personal friend, and I was threatened with a multimillion-dollar lawsuit as a result of that same case.

My experience is hardly unique. Thousands of Christian students are graduating into a work world that is as unbalanced as their public school or their secular college. Students are no longer liberated by graduation; instead they move from one state of legal disadvantage to another. Christians—particularly Christians who seek to evangelize at work—find that they sometimes have less freedom at work than they did at school. Employers, fearful of lawsuits, will often prohibit or even punish communication of religious ideas. The same agents of "diversity" and "tolerance" that oppress high school and college students are often active in the workplace, mandating religiously offensive "sensitivity training" and preaching views of sexuality, gender, and race that are incompatible with evangelical Christianity.

Imagine you've graduated from college or graduate school and are enjoying a new, lucrative career at a large company. You have developed friendships with several coworkers and have an excellent relationship with your secretary, a young woman. As you get to know your new friends better and as you work long hours together, your talks sometimes become more serious. You know that Brian's marriage is in trouble, Kevin's parents passed away when he was very young, and Lisa is engaged to a man she is not sure she wants to marry. Your friends know that you are a Christian, and they know that you volunteer with your church's youth ministry. Good-naturedly, they mock your relative righteousness, and you tease them back. Occasionally, you have serious conversations. One evening Lisa even asked you to pray for her, and you report these developments to your home Bible study group, convinced that the Lord is beginning to work through you.

One afternoon, late, your secretary comes in your office, obviously troubled. You are concerned, and although it is slightly unprofessional, you close your office door and ask her if anything is wrong. Nancy is your friend, after all. She tells you that her boyfriend wants to move out, and she doesn't know what to do. They fight all the time, but they still love each other. She tearfully asks your advice.

Your response is honest. In the most compassionate words you can muster, you tell her that living together before marriage is not really in

God's plan. You tell her that perhaps he should move out, and maybe she should consider going to church with him—starting over. You offer to "double-date" to your church. You'll take your girlfriend, and Nancy will take her boyfriend. You don't use any words such as sin, and you certainly don't say that Nancy is going to hell because of her disobedience. Nancy seems to respond positively to you. She does not take you up on the church offer, but she definitely does not seem offended. You even report the conversation to your Bible study as further evidence of God's move at your office.

You and Nancy don't speak again about the issue. Work has grown busy, and you are traveling a lot. It's not that you don't want to follow up on your conversation, but there just hasn't been an appropriate time. However, you really want to talk with Nancy. Brian told you that her boyfriend has moved out, and she's been in a state of depression ever since. Lisa tells you that Nancy's even taking an antidepressant.

Nancy's work begins to suffer. Three days after she forgets to ship out a crucial FedEx package, you fill out Nancy's annual performance review. Although you think the review is generally good, you are critical of some aspects of her performance. Overall, you rate her a 7 on the 10-point scale. In the "comments" section at the bottom of the evaluation, you write: "Nancy is an outstanding secretary. However, she's struggled some in recent weeks. I think she may be letting personal problems impact her work performance."

One Monday morning—two weeks after you turned in Nancy's evaluation—you arrive at work to see Nancy's desk empty. Her nameplate is gone, and her computer is off. What happened? Puzzled, you walk into your office and turn on your computer. You intend to send an E-mail to the office manager, asking about Nancy. You open your E-mail program and notice that you have a message, marked "urgent," from human resources. The text is simple: "Please see me as soon as you arrive this morning. Thank you." The message is from the company's local director of human resources. Puzzled, you get up and walk to her office.

She doesn't smile when you arrive. She doesn't even get up from behind her desk. "Take a seat." Her voice is stern. "We've got a problem."

"What is it? Nancy?"

"Yes, it's Nancy. Have you been expecting my message? Did you know she was going to complain?"

Now you are truly confused. "Complain? About what?"

"About what?" The director's voice rises. "Nancy has filed a harassment complaint against you."

You are dumbfounded. "Sexual harassment? I've never . . ."

She cuts you off. "No, religious harassment. According to her statement, one evening approximately two months ago, you asked her into your office and asked her to discuss her personal life. When she told you that she was having problems with her boyfriend, you told her that her relationship with her boyfriend was not God's will and asked her to come to church with you. She refused to go. After she refused, you began talking to her less and filled out a negative performance review that explicitly singles out her personal life as the reason for her poor review."

The director pauses, as if looking for a response, but you don't have one. She continues. "Since the complaint was made, the HR staff has conducted a confidential investigation. We have found that you frequently discuss your religious beliefs with employees and sometimes even mock their personal moral choices." She pushes a pen and blank notebook toward you. "I'll need a statement from you responding to the charges. We need to know whether you admit or deny the accusations. In the meantime, Nancy has been transferred out of your department. You are not permitted to speak to her. In fact, don't even look at her. Also, it would behoove you to cut back your proselytization efforts. They are not welcome and are offensive to your coworkers."

You stare at the blank piece of paper and pick up the pen. Just as you start writing, you ask a question, "Will I need a lawyer?"

The director turns away from you and begins typing on her computer. "You can use my phone if you want to call one now."

The Rise of Religious Harassment

Virtually every American adult is familiar with sexual harassment. Your workplace most likely has an explicit sexual harassment policy, and you may even know someone who has either suffered through sexual harassment or been accused of sexual harassment. Sexual harassment allegations are routinely the subject of news stories, television shows, and movies. There's hardly a sane American male who doesn't have at least some fear of sexual harassment allegations when (or if) he asks a coworker for a date.

Although the work culture is saturated with information about sexual harassment, very few individuals are aware of its legal origins. They know only that sexual harassment is against the law. They do not know how or why it is illegal. And they almost certainly do not know that the same law that bans sexual harassment is now sometimes used to prevent employers and employees from even speaking about their faith while at work.

Title VII of the Civil Rights Act of 1964—a law passed in response to endemic racism in the South and elsewhere—bars private employers from discriminating against their employees on the basis of race, sex, or religion. The early, conventional reading of this statute was that it prevented employers from firing (or refusing to hire) an employee simply because he or she was black, female, or Muslim. The law extended not just into hiring and firing but also promotions and on-the-job conduct.

Chrysler, for example, cannot hire women and then refuse to promote them. It cannot hire Hispanics, then confine them all to assembly-line work.

As the law developed and more women and minorities entered the workforce, the concept of "harassment" emerged. Just as it was discriminatory to refuse to hire or promote someone because he was black, it was also discriminatory to subject him to ridicule or mockery because of his race. If the "harassment" became so severe or pervasive that it was essentially a "term or condition of employment," then the law was violated. If a person is harassed because of her race, or because of her sex, then the law considers that harassment to be discrimination.

In the last decade harassment litigation has exploded. Companies now spend billions of dollars a year defending themselves against harassment allegations. Prominent companies have paid hundreds of millions of dollars in judgments and settlements to allegedly harassed plaintiffs. My own law firm employs more than a dozen highly paid attorneys who do nothing but defend companies against harassment allegations.

As a consequence of this litigation explosion (and the attendant publicity), two things have occurred. First, companies have begun to clamp down on their employees by not just prohibiting actions that are actually harassing but also prohibiting actions that might lead to harassment. For example, several companies bar employees from dating each other—under any circumstances. While asking for a date is not, by itself, harassment, companies are aware that dating can lead to offensive conduct. In many offices sexual jokes are banned completely, downloading pornography or bringing pornography to work is a fireable offense, and the utterance of any kind of racial epithet or joke results in immediate termination.

Christians have tended to approve of most of these developments. We don't want to work in sexually charged environments, and the thought of a workplace that permits even the slightest hints of racist expression offends us. In a real way, the rise of harassment litigation has resulted in a cleaner, safer workplace.

There is, however, a dark side. As many legal commentators have noted, since we spend the lion's share of our waking hours at work, the workplace is our primary avenue of speech and interaction. These anti-harassment guidelines, though usually well-intentioned, directly prohibit speech that others *might* consider offensive. If an employer takes the position that it will flatly ban offensive speech from the workplace, then religious speech is directly imperiled.

Because Title VII bars discrimination on the basis of race, sex, and *religion,* all of the antiharassment rules and guidelines that apply to racial and sexual harassment could, in theory, apply to religious harassment. Although few of us would weep for an employee fired because he consistently called his coworker, Ahmed, a "filthy terrorist Muslim," harassment complaints often arise not when one person is explicitly derogatory but when the other person is subjectively offended. History and experience tell us that religious speech is fraught with peril. Even pleasant religious conversations can turn difficult quickly, with evangelism being particularly dangerous. When you witness to another person, even if you avoid all traces of fundamentalism or judgmentalism and are more compassionate than the most moist-eyed, guitar-strumming pastor of a "seeker church," you are essentially telling that person you know a better way. If your way is better, then their way is worse. That is not always a welcome message. In fact, just the very name of Christ is not always welcome.

While religious harassment claims are not nearly as prevalent as sexual or racial harassment claims, lawsuits, court rulings, and company policies that were unthinkable even ten years ago are cropping up with depressing regularity. Consider the following examples:[1]

- A Pennsylvania court held that religious statements in the company newsletter and Bible verses printed on company checks were religious harassment.[2]
- The Oregon unemployment commissioner ruled that it is religious harassment to permit a Seventh-Day Adventist employee to discuss his religion in the office.[3]
- The Oregon unemployment commissioner also found that it is religious harassment for a manager to tell an employee that some of his personal habits are immoral.[4]
- An Iowa county government instructed an employee to refrain from any activity that "could be construed as religious proselytizing, witnessing or counseling" and instructed him to remove from his office any items having a religious connotation, including a desk Bible.[5]
- A division of the California Department of Education bans employees from engaging in any religious discussions in the workplace and prohibits the display or promotion of any religious materials outside the workplace.[6]
- A federal court issued an injunction barring the defendant and any of his employees from making any religious remarks contrary to their fellow employees' religious beliefs.[7]
- A major airline's internal policies (later withdrawn) forbade any material or comments with "religious overtones, whether positive or negative."[8]

If practicing law has taught me anything, it is that there is an immutable law of the legal universe, one more potent, perhaps, than any of Newton's laws of motion: *If the law allows lawsuits, lawsuits will be filed.* In other words, if legal developments open up new avenues of litigation, there will *always* be lawyers and litigants who will take advantage of those new possibilities. With respect to religious harassment, because courts have sanctioned Christians for proselytizing, or for merely speaking, we can expect more litigation. There is no shortage of potential plaintiffs—individuals offended by Christians or Christianity—and there will be no shortage of lawyers to take their cases.

For too long Christians have sat on the sidelines and watched basic free speech rights be decimated in the workplace. Because we were offended by much of the speech that was banned, we cheered new legal developments, or at the very least watched with little concern. Now, a legal doctrine (Title VII) that was once intended to protect religious workers is used to shield the public from religion.

While it is true that religious harassment claims are far from rampant, it is important to note that a legal framework now exists that can be used to stifle religious speech on a grand scale. The fact that systematic repression has not yet occurred is more a reflection of a society that still tends to value its religious citizens than it is evidence of a legal system that protects religious expression.

Workplace Indoctrination

At the same time that legal developments are resulting in increasing restrictions on employee religious speech, cultural and political developments are increasingly turning employers into one more mouthpiece for the church of the left. While an employer may not speak with a religious voice without "harassing" its workers, it is often encouraged to indoctrinate its workers in modern ideologies of tolerance and diversity.

Perhaps the most notorious example of workplace indoctrination is the case of John Rocker, the most famous relief pitcher in America. The nation's sports fans were first introduced to the pitcher (for the Atlanta Braves at the time) during the 1999 National League

Championship Series. Rocker would sprint from the bull pen to the pitcher's mound, yell at fans, and pump his fists with every strikeout. He loved taunting the opposition and insulting the fans, and he even criticized his own teammates. A loudmouthed, trash-talking fan of the World Wrestling Federation, he seemed to be the poster boy for the modern boorish athlete. America, however, is full of boorish athletes. He was certainly not the worst-behaving baseball player, nor was he the most interesting or outrageous. In short, he was just another cocky kid with a cannon arm.

That was before the winter of 1999–2000. During the off season, *Sports Illustrated* asked a reporter to do a story on John Rocker. During the course of the interview, Rocker made several offensive and racist statements. He mocked gays, drug addicts, single mothers, and Asian drivers. He called a black teammate a "fat monkey." It was almost as if Rocker went through a checklist of every significant minority group in the country, insulting each one.

When I first heard his comments, I was appalled. Rocker's statements were disgusting. However, I couldn't say that I was surprised. His off-season comments seemed accurately to reflect his on-field demeanor. By that time, I was used to athletes misbehaving and no longer expected them to serve as role models for me or my children. If you pay attention to the sports news wires, you'll note hardly a week goes by without hearing about a prominent professional or college athlete beating his wife or girlfriend, soliciting a prostitute, committing sexual assault or rape, and sometimes committing murder. Since Rocker's ill-fated comments, the country has faced two murder trials involving NFL football players, the sexual assault trial of a former All-Pro tight end of the Green Bay Packers, and numerous spouse abuse incidents. We've also seen athletes charge into stands physically to attack fans, verbally attack fans with vile racial epithets, and produce profanity and bigotry-laden rap albums.

None of these individuals, however, is as infamous as John Rocker. I was stunned by the reaction he generated. Overnight he was the subject of countless talk shows and television news reports. Civil rights activists protested his comments, and fans (particularly in New York) called for his head. Within days he became one of the most reviled men in America.

Though I was puzzled by the level of vitriol directed at Rocker (I wondered why his stupid comments were more deserving of public ridicule than wife-beating, rape, and murder), I was not overly concerned by the public reaction. If individuals want to express outrage at a relief pitcher, then that is their right. Disproportionate anger and irrational responses are just part of the cost of a free society. However, what did disturb me was his employer's response—the response of Major League Baseball. Rocker was slapped with one of the longest suspensions in baseball history, he was fined thousands of dollars, and he was ordered to undergo psychological counseling and sensitivity training. When this punishment was announced, most Americans barely blinked. Some wanted even more severe punishment; others thought it was just about right. Almost no one, however, saw the employer's response for what it was—a grave threat to freedom.

Think for a moment about what happened. An employee on vacation expressed personal opinions to a reporter on several topics that had nothing to do with the subject of his employment. Those opinions were hateful and controversial, but they were not given within the scope of his employment, and no sane person would think that they reflected the opinions of the Atlanta Braves or of Major League Baseball. They were just the ravings of one prejudiced individual.

Then think about the response. As a condition for continuing his career, in addition to paying fines and sitting out a long suspension, Rocker was required to submit to psychological counseling and *sensitivity training.* In other words, he was to submit to employer-directed moral indoctrination.

As so often happens, the bad acts of an unsympathetic individual helped open the door of respectability to truly repressive practices. If an employer can require psychological counseling and reeducation for off-the-job insults, why not for controversial, "offensive" off-the-job statements of moral principles or religious beliefs? Just this past year, the National Basketball Association and the New York Knicks publicly censured point guard Charlie Ward when he was quoted as making controversial statements regarding the role of Jews in Christ's death and the negative reactions of some Jewish individuals when family members or friends convert to Christianity. And it would be easy to imagine punishment for other "offensive" or "discriminatory" statements such as women should submit to their husbands or extramarital sexual behavior is sinful.

While most of us will never be in positions where anyone will listen to our public statements, much less print them in the newspaper, the John Rocker case does shed light on a practice that will have increasing relevance for even the most low-level corporate employee—employee sensitivity training. As civil rights and antiharassment lawsuits proliferate, leftist activists increasingly call for companies to take proactive steps to stamp out discrimination. Corporations now hire "inclusion officers" and require diversity training for incoming employees. If individual employees are accused of sexist or racist behavior, they are often subjected to mandatory diversity and sensitivity counseling sessions. A key component of race or sex discrimination settlements is often the creation or expansion of sensitivity training efforts. These training or counseling sessions are often nothing more than tent revivals for leftist identity and sexual politics.

If diversity training were nothing more than an admonition that racism, sexism, and homophobia are undesirable workplace traits that could place you and your company in significant legal jeopardy, then there would be little cause for alarm. However, a survey of leading diversity trainers reveals that the agenda is much more ambitious. One leading diversity consultant, the Kaleel Jamison Consulting Group, lists as one of its primary goals nothing less than "culture change." According to Kaleel Jamison, it is not enough to teach employees and companies to "build inclusion" and "leverage diversity" because it is "the right thing to do." Instead, the employer must work for "strategic culture change."[9]

Toward that end, Kaleel Jamison seeks to transform employee racial perceptions and, in particular, transform white employees' understandings of their own race and role in identity politics. Kaleel Jamison promotes a "white awareness" that helps whites understand their own "privilege and prejudice" and helps them "understand oneself as a white person." The goal is nothing less than a fundamental reunderstanding of race, racial differences, and racial activism.

Other organizations endorse and distribute documents called the *Whiteness Papers,*[10] with titles such as "Decentering Whiteness" and "White Men and the Denial of Racism." One paper, called "White Antiracist Activism," notes that white privilege "saturates our society" and speaks against white people's tendency to "falsely claim all have equal opportunity." Another paper offers a defense of affirmative action and a rebuttal of "mythical" and "fanciful" thinking that leads white men to ask questions such as "What privilege?", "Why do we have to keep talking about racism?", and "What happened to 'the best man wins'?"

With respect to sexual orientation, the message is explicit. I had the privilege of viewing a popular diversity presentation that began by showing a picture of the "new face of discrimination in America." The presenter flashed a slide of a handsome young man. With his voice quivering, he said. "This is my son, and he is gay." He then commenced a sixty-minute, impassioned diatribe against "heterosexism," saying that true nondiscrimination means acceptance, tolerance, and understanding. The speech was laced with implicit and explicit insults of religious views that condemned homosexual behavior.

DiversityCentral.com, a Web-based clearinghouse for diversity training materials, featured a series of articles on sexual orientation in the workplace.[11] One article suggests taking employees through a tour of the "dynamics of human sexuality" that covers "biological sex, gender identification, gender roles, sexual orientation, sexual orientation identification identity, homophobia and heterosexism." During this tour, which the author called "quite the eye opener," the teacher or facilitator is to instruct the students in the alleged differences between our biological sex and our gender identity. In other words, a person can be a biological woman with a male gender identity.

The tour also teaches that

- "A boy is completely aware of his [sexual] orientation by age thirteen.
- For girls the average age of awareness is between fifteen/seventeen.
- There are four sexual orientations currently identified:
    1. Heterosexual: physical and/or emotional attraction to persons of the opposite sex.
    2. Homosexual: physical and/or emotional attraction to persons of same sex.
    3. Bisexual: physical and/or emotional attraction to persons regardless of sex.
    4. Asexual: tendency not to become attracted to others regardless of sex."

Clearly then, diversity training is about much more than merely training employees to value other workers and treat them with respect.

It is about teaching a new understanding of race, gender, and sexuality. It is a continuation of the identity politics and moral reeducation that have consumed universities and are infecting our public schools. The church of the left now reaches into our workplaces.

And the law allows it. You may believe that it is discriminatory to force Christian individuals to attend training seminars or counseling sessions that are, in essence, moral education sessions. You may believe that the law—if it sometimes prevents employers and employees from even speaking about Christianity—would prohibit this level of indoctrination.

Although I do not know of any cases that have directly challenged an employer's ability to mandate sensitivity training, I have little doubt that such a challenge would lose. Since 1977, the Supreme Court has interpreted Title VII's protections against religious discrimination to provide only minimal protections to employees who seek exemptions from corporate work requirements. In *TWA v. Hardison,*[12] the Supreme Court held that the antidiscrimination provisions of Title VII did not require an employer to bear anything more than a *de minimis* cost to accommodate religious observers because any greater cost would impose an "undue hardship" on the employer's business.

As a result of this case, workers requesting routine Sabbath exemptions from work requirements are lawfully rejected, even when other employees agree to switch shifts or cover job responsibilities. In 1986, the Supreme Court went even further, reducing worker religious rights to the point of irrelevance. In the case of *Ansonia Board of Education v. Philbrook,*[13] the Court examined the case of Ron Philbrook, a high school teacher whose religious beliefs (he was a member of the World Wide Church of God) prevented him from working on certain holy days. The Ansonia Board of Education had a policy prohibiting the taking of personal leave for religious reasons after an employee had already been absent three days for mandatory religious observances. Philbrook proposed using his personal business days for religious observance, but the school refused. Philbrook was forced either to work on holy days or to take unauthorized, unpaid leave. Philbrook filed suit under Title VII.

The Supreme Court ruled against the teacher, holding that once an employer offers an accommodation (in this case, the three-day rule), then the employer is not required to implement an accommodation proposed by an employee even if it means that the employee will suffer financially. In other words, once an employer makes an accommodation offer, then that offer is the only accommodation required. In response to these cases, one commentator noted: "Title VII has been rendered largely meaningless as a source of protection for the religiously observant employee of the secular employer."[14]

The result of these legal developments, when combined with evolving antiharassment standards, is that Christian employees and employers in the secular workplace are at a distinct legal disadvantage. If a Christian supervisor implemented a mandatory morning Bible study, then he would be guilty of religious harassment. If a secular supervisor began a sexual orientation–related sensitivity training program, then not only would the law allow him to require his employees to attend; it would also permit him to refuse to excuse Christian (or other religious) participants. Two worldviews are held with religious zeal. One may use the secular workplace to preach its gospel; the other may not.

The answer to this disparity is not equalizing indoctrination. The answer is more freedom. We do not want a situation where State Farm employees are subject to mandatory Bible study, Prudential employees listen to diversity lectures, and Progressive workers go to company yoga and meditation sessions. Instead, we should seek a work world in which State Farm, Prudential, and Progressive sell insurance, while their workers conduct themselves respectfully and have the freedom to be Christian or Muslim, gay or straight.

We do not have the legal or political strength to "liberate" employers to indoctrinate their workers with a Christian message. Public and, more important, judicial opinion will not support such a move. However, we do have the strength to argue for and practice freedom. We should fight the expansion of antiharassment regulations, and we should fight to expand the right of workers to obtain reasonable accommodations for religious observances. Personally, in our own workplaces, we should continue to witness as the Lord leads, regardless of fear or heavy-handed corporate policies. Additionally, we should not be quick to take offense. Every frivolous or sensitive complaint that we make chips away at the freedom that we need. Unless you truly are subjected to malicious, oppressive insults or true sexual or racial harassment, do not contribute to the culture of victimization.

Christ and His disciples suffered much for the gospel, and so can we. However, neither Christ nor His disciples allowed themselves to be muzzled. Perhaps, as thousands of Christians not only proclaim the gospel with boldness but also sacrificially protect the right of others to be just as bold—even for causes that we dislike—we can begin to turn the tide away from indoctrination and back toward the freedom under which the gospel flourishes.

8

The Sounds
of Freedom

In the fog, bitterness, and confusion of the culture war, we often lose sight of ourselves and our principles. We begin to think that since we are on the side of God, any decision that favors us must be good and any opposition must be evil. We sometimes demand more than just equality, more than just freedom of expression, detouring into the nostril-flaring rage so indicative of those who consider themselves the "chosen ones."

In one of my most disturbing cases, I represented yet another church before a county zoning board. A neighbor had complained to the local board, asking that the church's conditional use permit be revoked. In other words, the neighbor wanted the church to be kicked off its property entirely. The church members were outraged—shocked at the religious persecution they were enduring. I took the case, eager to help brothers and sisters in need.

Then I learned more about the case. It turned out that the neighbor was complaining not because she hated Christianity or despised Pentecostal Christians but because the church *had not complied with a single one of the conditions* on its conditional use permit. In fact, it had used part of the church grounds as a trash dump and had parked junked cars and old trucks in prominent places near the neighbor's home and property. At one point the church kept a roaming band of chickens on the property! The church had created a terrible eyesore and was doing nothing either to improve the grounds or to comply with the conditional use permit.

When the board meeting came, my strategy was simple: I was going to grovel. I apologized on behalf of the church, and I apologized on behalf of the members. I begged the board for a second chance, and I asked the neighbor to forgive us for our negligence. I begged, pleaded, and argued for almost four full hours. Finally, by the closest possible vote, the board gave the church a second chance.

I expected that the church members would be grateful. Some were, but most were outraged. They couldn't believe that the board had said such "evil things" to a *church*. They were sputtering with rage at the neighbor, who was so obviously opposing God's work. And several were upset with me, demanding to know why I had apologized, why I had not stood stronger for the church.

At first I was angry at their reaction, indignant that they could not see how wrong they had been and how close they had come to losing their church. I was also ashamed that a neighbor was seeing the ugly side of church—the sense of entitlement and self-righteousness that so easily creeps into our attitudes and actions. This church had not been persecuted. It had been oppressing its neighbor and flaunting the law.

Too often, in seemingly benign ways, we Christians oppress our neighbors and flaunt fair and reasonable laws. We want the government on *our* side and against the infidels. We do not care if friends and neighbors will be offended by government prayer or workplace indoctrinations. So long as it is Christian prayer and Christian indoctrination, then our cause is just.

How wrong we are. If you paid close attention to the stories in this book, or if you pay close attention to the stories of religious persecution around the country, you should notice something important. Though national legal structures are unbalanced, the Supreme Court is not directly discriminating against us, Congress is not directly discriminating against us, and neither is the president. Though they have all had a hand in creating legal doctrines that make discrimination possible, they are not the ones shutting down youth ministries or graphically using state authority to advocate homosexuality and ridicule Christianity. Nor are they kicking Christian student groups off campus. The people directly attacking us are our friends and neighbors: our fellow students, our teachers, and our local politicians. Those are the people who most directly attack us, and those are the people we most need to reach.

When we seek special rights for Christians, when we ask the government to pray for us, we alienate those friends, neighbors, teachers, and politicians. When we focus all of our efforts on top-down change—through Supreme Court rulings, presidential races, and congressional enactments—we become not agents of freedom but just another voice of indoctrination.

However, when we abandon any pretense of seeking governmental favor and instead seek only freedom and equality, we become agents of reconciliation and healing. During the two short years that I've been focused on campus religious freedom issues, I have formed real and lasting friendships with atheists, Jews, liberals, and libertarians. These friendships could never have formed if I had focused instead on school prayer or fighting for the "right" of secular employers to mandate Bible studies or prayer meetings. By standing for freedom, I have the ability to know and minister to people who would otherwise shun and persecute me.

In short, we must give up some things that are precious to us in order to gain opportunities to minister and liberate. We must give up symbols of our beliefs and of our nation's heritage to gain the ability to reach *this* nation, *this* people, at *this* time. As we stand for freedom, we will gain the credibility to fight the oppression and indoctrination that characterize too many of our public schools, secular universities, and private workplaces. By giving up the fight for "special" rights, we gain incalculable advantage in the battle for equality—for a level playing field.

Many on the left and the right see the fight as either/or. Either we advance our agenda in high schools, in college, and at work, or the other side will. I say, let no one appropriate the power of government to advance a moral agenda. The answer is not either/or. The answer is neither. Neither the right nor the left own the schools, and neither Christians, nor Muslims, nor atheists, nor Jews, nor leftists, nor anyone can appropriate the reins of power to force their moral agenda down the throats of America's citizens.

In the fight for freedom and equality, we have much work to do. The structures of government now disfavor Christianity and lie fully open to use by the church of the left. Think of two individuals, both equally committed to their worldviews. One is an evangelical Christian; the other is a secular leftist. The secular liberal could become a teacher in a public school and "evangelize" her students to the fullest extent. The liberal could teach visions of gender, sex, and race that are at odds with Christianity, Judaism, Islam, and virtually every other major religion. She could bring performers into class that would mock Christians and advance a sexually permissive lifestyle. In college, she would find herself surrounded by like-minded students and faculty. She would even find that in some schools she could lead movements to kick Christians off campus and remove their voice entirely. In the workplace, she could use her employer to advance her agenda. She could lead "sensitivity" classes that again contradict basic Christian teachings and, with a single word of complaint, she could label her Christian coworkers as harassers and silence their voices. At no time in her life would she be guaranteed that anyone would actually believe and embrace her message, but at every stage she would have the right to speak and the power to compel others to listen.

Contrast this with the evangelical Christian. Although she could form a Christian club in high school and even become a public high school teacher, she could not use her classroom to advocate Christianity. She would be subjected to reeducation and intimidation in most every secular university, and some would even seek to exclude her. When she joined the workforce, her ability to witness to fellow employees often would depend entirely on the good will of her coworkers. If even one complained, then she might be silenced. At no point could she form a Bible study and require any person to attend. In other words, at no time would she be able to harness the reins of power to compel others to listen to her message, and at virtually every stage of life she would face the very real possibility that those in power would seek to silence her completely. However, unlike the leftist, if she were able to speak—if she were able to communicate the gospel—she would be guaranteed that it would bear fruit. The Word will not return void (Isa. 55:11).

That promise is our greatest hope. If we can only open our mouths, then the Lord will prevail. We may never win over the nation, and we may never win over the world, but we will save lives and touch hearts.

I am not sure if Tufts Christian Fellowship won any new converts during its battle for survival, but I know they touched at least one heart. I will never forget the moments after the climactic hearing before the student Judiciary. After almost eight hours of spiritual and intellectual warfare, I was drained. I walked out of the hearing room through the lines of protesters feeling despair and self-doubt. Some of the senior leaders were in tears. As we walked back to the InterVarsity house, we talked about the hearing, made guesses about the outcome, and relived some of the most dramatic moments. Two blocks from the house, one of the senior leaders wondered if anyone would be there waiting for us. "They said that they would pray and worship until we finished, but they also thought the hearing would last only two hours. It's been six hours since they expected us back."

"I bet a few are still hanging around." I offered a reassuring guess and we trudged on down the road. A block later, about one hundred yards from the house, I caught the unmistakable sound of dozens of young voices lifted up in praise to God.

I looked at the senior leaders. Their downcast faces suddenly flickered with hope, their eyes shining. "Do you hear them? They're still praising!"

The leaders practically ran back into the house. When the door flew open, we saw the entire group, still praising with all their hearts. They exploded with joy when we came in. Although the outcome was still in doubt, they cheered us and praised God even more. They did not know if their group would survive, and they knew they would face ridicule and mockery in the coming days, but they were full of love for their Savior and were serving Him with all their hearts.

To this day, when I close my eyes, I can hear the sound of their singing—the sound of joyful voices praising God. I can also hear the sound of the Trinity youth, praising God in their Spirit Life Center. That is the sound that we must all fight to hear. That is the sound of true freedom.

NOTES

In general, I am deeply indebted to the following works for helping me understand the scope of modern liberalism: Christina Hoff Summers, *The War Against Boys: How Misguided Feminism Is Harming Our Young Men,* Simon & Schuster (2000); Alan Charles Kors and Harvey L. Silverglate, *The Shadow University: The Betrayal of Liberty on America's Campuses,* Free Press (1998); David Brooks, *Bobos in Paradise: The New Upper Class and How They Got There,* Touchstone Books (2000); and Sally Soltel, *PC, M.D.: How Political Correctness Is Corrupting Medicine,* Basic Books (2000). I am also indebted to the writers and editors of *National Review, National Review Online,* the *Weekly Standard,* and the *New Republic*—magazines that are invaluable resources for helping comprehend larger cultural and political trends. This is not a book that relied on Christian sources. Instead, I attempted to examine the legal and political culture from the perspective of the actual decision-makers—individuals and institutions that are rarely (if ever) explicitly evangelical or even Christian.

Throughout the book I quote conversations that I had with judges, other students, teachers, lawyers, and so on. These conversations do not purport to be exact, word-for-word renditions of those conversations but are instead my best recollection of the conversations. I have placed these recollections in conversation form to help the reader experience these cultural battles as I experienced them.

ENDNOTES

Chapter 2

1. All quotes and news regarding Clarence Thomas's invitation to speak to the Davis Levin First Amendment Conference are taken from Robert M. Rees, "The Annals of Liberalism," *Honolulu Weekly,* 22 June 2001.

2. Quotes and concepts regarding faith-equivalent liberalism are taken from Stanley Kurtz, "The Faith-Based Left: Getting Behind the Debate," *National Review Online,* www.nationalreview.com 5 February 2001, and Stanley Kurtz, "The Church of the Left: Finding Meaning in Liberalism," *National Review Online,* 31 May 2001.

3. Kurtz, "The Church of the Left," *National Review Online,* 31 May 2001.

Chapter 3

1. Quotes regarding the trials of Massachusetts parents and the "Teach Out" conference at Tufts University are taken from "Kids Get Graphic Instruction in Homosexual Sex," *Massachusetts News,* 5 June 2000. For more information about these incidents, contact Scott Whiteman at the Parents' Rights Coalition of Massachusetts, P.O. Box 175, Newton Massachusetts 02466. Also found at www.massnews.com.

2. Ibid.

3. Ibid.

4. Ibid.

5. The Hot, Sexy and Safer case can be read at *Brown v. Hot, Sexy and Safer Productions, Inc.,* 68 F.3d 525 (1st Cir. 1995).

6. The Wiccan textbook case can be read at *Brown v. Woodland Joint Unified School District,* 27 F.3d 1373 (9th Cir. 1994).

7. The Lemon case can be read at *Lemon v. Kurtzman,* 403 U.S. 602 (1971).

8. *Cantwell v. Connecticut,* 310 U.S. 296 (1940).

9. *Sherbert v. Verner,* 374 U.S. 398 (1963).

10. *Employment Division v. Smith,* 494 U.S. 872 (1990).

11. *Welsh v. United States,* 398 U.S. 333 (1970).

12. *Torcaso v. Watkins,* 367 U.S. 488 (1961).

13. *Frazee v. Illinois Department of Employment Security,* 489 U.S. 829 (1989).

14. *Thomas v. Review Board of Indiana Employment Security Division,* 450 U.S. 707 (1981).

15. As justification for the statement that more teenagers are attending prayer meetings than using hard drugs, compare the estimate from SYATP.com's 19 September 2001 press release that nearly three million American students participated in See You at the Pole in September 2001 with the 1998 National Household Survey on Drug Abuse's estimate that 1.1 million youths ages 12–17 were dependent on illicit drugs (estimate can be found at www.drugfreeschools.com). See 1999 and 2000 results of this survey at www.drugabusestatistics.samsha.gov.

16. *Lamb's Chapel v. Center Moriches School District,* 508 U.S. 384 (1993).

17. Stephen Dinan, "Cultural Faceoff Centers on Schools," *Washington Times,* 26 December 2000.

18. Evangelical Christians are defined by the following faith criteria: "Those included in this segment [evangelical Christianity] meet the criteria for being born again; say their faith is very important in their life today; believe they have a personal responsibility to share their religious beliefs about Christ with non-Christians; believe that Satan

exists; believe that eternal salvation is possible only through grace, not works; believe that Jesus Christ lived a sinless life on earth; and describe God as the all-knowing, all-powerful, perfect deity who created the universe and still rules it today." They represent only 8 percent of the population of the United States. Although 41 percent of the population classifies itself as "born again" (a very broad term), almost half of born-again Christians do not believe Satan is a living being, and fully 26 percent of born-again Christians believe that it doesn't matter what faith you follow because "they all teach the same lessons." Source: Barna Research Institute,

19. Vignettes relating student ignorance of Christianity are taken from Jay D. Wexler, "Beyond the 'New Consensus': Teaching About Religion and the Challenges of Civic Education" (publication forthcoming). Mr. Wexler's source for the North Carolina incident is Warren A. Nord, *Religion & American Education: Rethinking a National Dilemma* (Raleigh, N.C.: The University of North Carolina Press, 1995), 199–200. His source for the Massachusetts high school example is Arthur Gilbert, "Reactions and Resources," *Religion and Public Education* (Theodore R. Sizer, ed. 1967). His source for the Eastern Washington University survey is Kelly McBride, "Religion Left Out at Schools Leery of Controversy, Many Teachers Shun Topic," *The Spokesman Review,* 1 September 1996.

Further citations for various free exercise cases:
Church of the Lukumi Babalu Aye, Inc. v. Hialeah, 508 U.S. 520 (1993).
United States v. Seeger, 380 U.S. 163 (1965).

Chapter 4

1. For a complete listing of Tufts University's recognized student organizations, see www.Tufts.edu.

2. Michael Paulson, "Campus Faith Groups Face Rebuke on Gay Rights," *Boston Globe,* 29 April 2000.

3. Ibid.

4. Michael Paulson, "Tufts Lifts Its Ban on Christian Group," *Boston Globe,* 17 May 2000.

5. Ibid.

6. Ibid.

For a sampling of other articles detailing or describing the battle at Tufts University, see Julia Duin, "Christian Ministry Caught Up in Rights Battle on Campus," *Washington Times,* 16 May 2000; Kathryn Jean Lopez, "Tufts to Be a Christian on Campus: Colleges Say Yes to Porn and No to God—but Not Without a Fight," *National Review Online,* 22 May 2000; Norah Vincent, "Welcome to the Club," *Village Voice,* December 27–January 2, 2001; and "Colloquy Live: Gay Rights vs. Religious Freedom," *Chronicle of Higher Education,* 11 May 2000.

Chapter 5

1. Quotes and examples of college orientation indoctrination taken from Alan Charles Kors, "Thought Reform 101," *Reason,* March 2000. Obtained online from www.thefire.org/reform.html.

2. Ibid.

3. For a complete listing of various censoring responses to David Horowitz's reparations advertisement, see http://frontpagemag.com/commentaries/2001/horowitz_censored.htm. This site provides links to original news articles and commentary regarding the widespread use of coercion, intimidation, and censorship on college campuses.

4. Other examples of college coercion taken from personal experience (Cornell and Harvard incidents) and from Alan Charles Kors and Harvey L. Silverglate, *The Shadow University: The*

Betrayal of Liberty on America's Campuses (New York: The Free Press, 1998).

5. *Boy Scouts of America v. Dale,* 530 U.S. 640 (2000).

Additional citations for cases dealing with religious freedom in public educational institutions are as follows:
Widmar v. Vincent, 454 U.S. 263 (1981).
Good News Club v. Milford Central School, 121 S.Ct. 2093 (2001).
Rosenberger v. University of Virginia, 515 U.S. 819 (1995).
University of Wisconsin v. Southworth, 529 U.S. 217 (2000).

Chapter 7

1. The following examples, as well as quoted commentary on the general state of Title VII protections of religious activity, can be found in the following articles: "Symposium, Religion in the Workplace: Proceedings of the 2000 Annual Meeting of the Association of American Law Schools Section of Law and Religion," 4 *Employee Rights and Employment Policy Journal,* 87 (2000) and Josh Schopf, "Religious Activity and Proselytization in the Workplace: The Murky Line Between Healthy Expression and Unlawful Harassment," 31 *Columbia Journal of Law and Social Problems,* 39 (Fall 1997).

2. A description of the Pennsylvania court's ban on religious articles in the company newsletter can be found in *Brown Transport v. Commonwealth of Pennsylvania,* 578 A.2d 555 (Pa. Cmwlth. 1990).

3. A description of the Oregon unemployment commissioner's action against the Seventh-Day Adventist can be found in *Oregon Commissioner of Bureau of Labor & Industry,* Case No. 29–90 (4 February 1991).

4. A description of the Oregon Bureau of Labor and Industries finding of religious harassment can be found in *Metebeke v. Bureau of Labor & Industries,* 903 P.2d 351 (Or. 1995).

5. A description of the Iowa county government's proselytization ban can be found in *Brown v. Polk County,* 61 F.3d 650 (8ᵗʰ Cir. 1995).

6. A description of the California Department of Education's anti-religious action can be found in *Tucker v. California,* 97 F.3d 1204 (9ᵗʰ Cir. 1996).

7. A description of the federal court injunction against comments contrary to other employees' religious beliefs can be found in *Turner v. Barr,* 806 F. Supp. 1025 (D.D.C. 1992).

8. A description of the airline's policy prohibiting religious comments can be found in "The Effect of the EEOC's Proposed Guidelines on Religion in the Workplace: Hearing Before the Subcommittee on Courts and Administrative Practice of the Senate Committee on the Judiciary," 103d Congress, 2d Session 1994, 151–152 (Statement of Earl Goode, Vice President, Alabama Christian Education Association).

9. Comprehensive descriptions of the Kaleel Jamison diversity program can be found at the company's Web site, www.kjcg.com: Particular attention should be paid to the sections entitled "Being Worthy," "Frequently Asked Questions," and "What Would You Do?"

10. The *Whiteness Papers* were distributed by an organization called the Center for the Study of White American Culture: A Multiracial Organization. Its Web site is www.euroamerican.org.

11. Liz Winfield, "Education on Sexual Orientation in the Workplace, Part II," The GilDeane Group (2000), published at www.diversity-central.com.

12. *TWA v. Hardison,* 432 U.S. 63 (1977).

13. *Ansonia Board of Education v. Philbrook,* 479 U.S. 60 (1986).

14. David L. Gregory, "Religious Harassment in the Workplace: An Analysis of the EEOC's Proposed Guideline," 56 *Montclair Law Review,* 119, 127 (1995).

ADDITIONAL RESOURCES

Throughout this book I have sought to provide legal information in a format that is engaging, interesting, and thought-provoking. However, when dealing with the law, there always comes a time when entertainment gives way to information. The appendices that follow are full of legal information—information that students and parents of students need.

Appendix A is taken from the United States Department of Education's *Guidelines on Religious Expression in Public Schools*. Appendix B is adapted from the Foundation for Individual Rights in Education's *Guide to Religious Liberty on Campus*. Both of these sources contain readable, reliable summaries of student religious rights. The Department of Education *Guidelines* focus on public secondary schools, and the Foundation for Individual Rights in Education's *Guide* is devoted to the college campus.

It is often said that knowledge is power. If you or your child is engaged in Christian activity in a public school or at college, it is imperative that you know and understand your legal rights. With that knowledge, you will know both the limits of your own expression and the limits of the state's power. School officials will be unable to intimidate you with misinformation. In fact, school officials often will cease persecution when confronted by a person who knows the law, shows them the law, and behaves according to the law. Though the pages that follow are admittedly not exciting to read, they do contain the knowledge you need.

APPENDIX A

(Excerpt from the Department of Education's *Guidelines on Religious Expression in Public Schools*)

Religious Expression in Public Schools

Student prayer and religious discussion: The Establishment Clause of the First Amendment does not prohibit purely private religious speech by students. Students therefore have the same right to engage in individual or group prayer and religious discussion during the school day as they do to engage in other comparable activity. For example, students may read their Bibles or other scriptures, say grace before meals, and pray before tests to the same extent they may engage in comparable nondisruptive activities. Local school authorities possess substantial discretion to impose rules of order and other pedagogical restrictions on student activities, but they may not structure or administer such rules to discriminate against religious activity or speech.

Generally, students may pray in a nondisruptive manner when not engaged in school activities or instruction, and subject to the rules that normally pertain in the applicable setting. Specifically, students in informal settings, such as cafeterias and hallways, may pray and discuss their religious views with each other, subject to the same rules of order as apply to other student activities and speech. Students may also speak to, and attempt to persuade, their peers about religious topics just as

191

they do with regard to political topics. School officials, however, should intercede to stop student speech that constitutes harassment aimed at a student or a group of students.

Students may also participate in before- or after-school events with religious content, such as "see you at the flag pole" gatherings, on the same terms as they may participate in other noncurriculum activities on school premises. School officials may neither discourage nor encourage participation in such an event.

The right to engage in voluntary prayer or religious discussion free from discrimination does not include the right to have a captive audience listen, or to compel other students to participate. Teachers and school administrators should ensure that no student is in any way coerced to participate in religious activity.

Graduation prayer and baccalaureates: Under current Supreme Court decisions, school officials may not mandate or organize prayer at graduation, nor organize religious baccalaureate ceremonies. If a school generally opens its facilities to private groups, it must make its facilities available on the same terms to organizers of privately sponsored religious baccalaureate services. A school may not extend preferential treatment to baccalaureate ceremonies and may in some instances be obliged to disclaim official endorsement of such ceremonies.

Official neutrality regarding religious activity: Teachers and school administrators, when acting in those capacities, are representatives of the state and are prohibited by the establishment clause from soliciting or encouraging religious activity, and from participating in such activity with students. Teachers and administrators also are prohibited from discouraging activity because of its religious content, and from soliciting or encouraging antireligious activity.

Teaching about religion: Public schools may not provide religious instruction, but they may teach *about* religion, including the Bible or other scripture: the history of religion, comparative religion, the Bible (or other scripture)-as-literature, and the role of religion in the history of the United States and other countries all are permissible public school subjects. Similarly, it is permissible to consider religious influences on art, music, literature, and social studies. Although public schools may teach about religious holidays, including their religious aspects, and may celebrate the secular aspects of holidays, schools may not observe holidays as religious events or promote such observance by students.

Student assignments: Students may express their beliefs about religion in the form of homework, artwork, and other written and oral assignments free of discrimination based on the religious content of their submissions. Such home and classroom work should be judged by ordinary academic standards of substance and relevance, and against other legitimate pedagogical concerns identified by the school.

Religious literature: Students have a right to distribute religious literature to their schoolmates on the same terms as they are permitted to distribute other literature that is unrelated to school curriculum or activities. Schools may impose the same reasonable time, place, and manner or other constitutional restrictions on distribution of religious literature as they do on nonschool literature generally, but they may not single out religious literature for special regulation.

Religious excusals: Subject to applicable State laws, schools enjoy substantial discretion to excuse individual students from lessons that are objectionable to the student or the students' parents on religious or other conscientious grounds. However, students generally do not have a Federal right to be excused from lessons that may be inconsistent with their religious beliefs or practices. School officials may neither encourage nor discourage students from availing themselves of an excusal option.

Released time: Subject to applicable State laws, schools have the discretion to dismiss students to off-premises religious instruction, provided that schools do not encourage or discourage participation or penalize those who do not attend. Schools may not allow religious instruction by outsiders on school premises during the school day.

Teaching values: Though schools must be neutral with respect to religion, they may play an active role with respect to teaching civic values and virtue, and the moral code that holds us together as a community. The fact that some of these values are held also by religions does not make it unlawful to teach them in school.

Student garb: Schools enjoy substantial discretion in adopting policies relating to student dress and school uniforms. Students generally have no federal right to be exempted from religiously neutral and generally applicable school dress rules based on their religious beliefs or practices; however, schools may not single out religious attire in general, or attire of a particular religion, for prohibition or regulation. Students may display religious messages on items of clothing to the same extent that they are permitted to display other comparable messages. Religious messages may not be singled out for suppression, but rather are subject to the same rules as generally apply to comparable messages.

The Equal Access Act

The Equal Access Act is designed to ensure that, consistent with the First Amendment, student religious activities are accorded the same access to public school facilities as are student secular activities. Based on decisions of the federal courts, as well as its interpretations of the Act, the Department of Justice has advised that the Act should be interpreted as providing, among other things, that:

General provisions: Student religious groups at public secondary schools have the same right of access to school facilities as is enjoyed by other comparable student groups. Under the Equal Access Act, a school receiving federal funds that allows one or more student noncurriculum-related clubs to meet on its premises during noninstructional time may not refuse access to student religious groups.

Prayer services and worship exercises covered: A meeting, as defined and protected by the Equal Access Act, may include a prayer service, Bible reading, or other worship exercise.

Equal access to means of publicizing meetings: A school receiving federal funds must allow student groups meeting under the Act to use the school media—including the public address system, the school newspaper, and the school bulletin board—to announce their meetings on the same terms as other noncurriculum-related student groups are allowed to use the school media. Any policy concerning the use of school media must be applied to all noncurriculum-related student groups in a nondiscriminatory matter. Schools, however, may inform students that certain groups are not school-sponsored.

Lunch-time and recess covered: A school creates a limited open forum under the Equal Access Act, triggering equal access rights for religious groups, when it allows students to meet during their lunch periods or other noninstructional time during the school day, as well as when it allows students to meet before and after the school day.

Revised May 1998

APPENDIX B

(Based on and adapted from the Foundation for Individual Rights in Education's upcoming *Guide to Religous Liberty on Campus*)

Religious Freedom in the Public University

For the public university student concerned with religious freedom, the Free Exercise Clause of the Constitution is much more critical than the Establishment Clause. (It is very unlikely that your public university will attempt to establish Lutheranism as an official religion, for example. It is likely, alas, that it will seek to restrict the free practice of a religion.) As explained above, the Free Exercise Clause protects religious individuals and groups from specifically targeted, anti-religious state action. In other words, a public university may not institute any policy designed primarily (or even partially) to suppress the practice of religion.

Again, as mentioned above, the Constitution also permits religious groups to "couple" their Free Exercise rights with other constitutional rights. In other words, if a religious individual or group is confronted with a university policy that discriminates against their religious message, then it may not only claim a violation of its Free Exercise rights but also of its rights to free speech and to free association. In such a circumstance, it becomes much more difficult for the university's policies to prevail.

Because of the symbiotic relationship of free speech, free association, and the free exercise of religion (a "symbiotic" relationship is one in which the parts of a relationship all strengthen and benefit each other), public universities are severely limited in their ability to regulate campus religious practice. The key word that governs a public university's obligations is *neutrality.* If it offers a benefit or access to individuals or organizations with a particular viewpoint or religion, then it must offer that same benefit or access to other individuals or organizations with different viewpoints or religions. The government may not engage in *viewpoint discrimination.*

Several major Supreme Court cases illustrate this principle. The first, *Widmar v. Vincent* (1981), held that once a university opens its facilities for use by a broad spectrum of student groups, it may not then deny religious organizations that same access.

This principle was reaffirmed in *Lamb's Chapel v. Center Moriches Union Free School* (1993), a case involving a public high school that denied religious organizations equal access to school facilities. The Supreme Court's conclusion was unanimous: "[I]t discriminates on the basis of viewpoint to permit school property to be used for the presentation of all views about family issues and child-rearing except those dealing with the subject matter from a religious standpoint."

Under the authority of *Widmar* and *Lamb's Chapel,* public universities that open gymnasiums, classrooms, auditoriums, and dorm facilities for use by groups as diverse as College Democrats, African-American Student Unions, anti-International Monetary Fund protest groups, feminists, and literary societies may not close those same facilities to religious organizations. Any university that attempts such discrimination is in clear violation of the law.

In fact, this principle of equal access is one of the most firmly established doctrines in constitutional law. In the summer of 2001, the Supreme Court ruled that public schools must offer equal access to religious groups not only in colleges and high schools, but also in *elementary schools.* This case, called *Good News Club v. Milford Central School,* firmly and definitively removes any doubt about religious students' access to public facilities. *Every* religious student or group at *every* level of schooling is entitled to the same access to school facilities as secular students or groups. If a school opens its facilities to political or cultural clubs, it cannot shut its doors in the face of religious students.

This principle of neutrality extends not only to the use of facilities, but also to the use of university funds. In *Rosenberger v. University of Virginia* (1995), the University of Virginia authorized payments from a Student Activities Fund for the printing costs of publications by certain student groups. This payment program was utilized by a wide variety of student groups to print a great diversity of publications espousing political, social, and even religious views. Although the university supported a wide range of groups, including Jewish and Shinto publications, it refused to support the publication of a Christian magazine.

In response, the Supreme Court found that the university was guilty of unconstitutional viewpoint discrimination: "Having offered to pay the third-party contractors on behalf of private speakers who convey their own messages, the University may not silence the expression of selected viewpoints."

In fact, *viewpoint neutrality* is an absolute precondition to any public funding for student organizations. In the case of *University of Wisconsin v. Southworth* (2000), the Supreme Court provided a perfect description of the neutrality requirement. In *Southworth,* a University of Wisconsin student challenged the University's mandatory student activity fee, alleging that to force him to fund student groups whose political and ideological speech he found offensive violated his First Amendment rights. Although the Supreme Court agreed that a mandatory fee involved the student's First Amendment rights, it held that those rights were protected *as long as the university allocated the funds on a neutral basis.* In Justice O'Connor's words: "Viewpoint neutrality is the justification for requiring the student to pay the fee in the first instance and for ensuring the integrity of the program's operation once the funds have been collected."

In sum, public universities that offer benefits to other "expressive organizations" on campus—an "expressive organization" exists, at least in part, for the purpose of expressing a particular viewpoint— may not deny the same benefit to students or groups simply because their viewpoint happens to be religious. This is a valuable application of the general principle—one might dub it the "Golden Rule" of constitutional decision-making—that citizens are entitled to equality before the law. That principle is one of the essential foundations of our liberty.

There is another form of legal jeopardy faced by campus religious organizations, however, that is unaffected by the "neutrality principle." Most contemporary legal attacks on religion make use of laws or regulations that were not, in fact, specifically designed to work against religion. These legal weapons instead are, for the most part, "neutral laws of general applicability" that simply are applied in ways that defeat religious practice. The perfect example, by its relevance for us, would be a university policy that prohibits discrimination on the basis of sexual orientation. A university would argue that its policy is simply a "neutral, general law" applicable to everyone: biology professors may not refuse to hire lesbian teaching assistants; the football team may not exclude gay linebackers; and campus religious organizations may not bar gay members. In other words, the rule was not designed to target a particular religion, or religion in general, but was instead created to protect all individuals from any discrimination based on sexual orientation.

The difference between this kind of situation and the situation faced by the religious individuals in *Widmar* and *Rosenberger* is obvious. The plaintiffs in those cases were attacking policies that were designed to benefit everyone *except* religious organizations. The viewpoint discrimination was clear. Most campus anti-discrimination policies are designed to apply to everyone, *including* religious organizations. In such a case, there appears to be no viewpoint discrimination whatsoever.

Prior to the Supreme Court's recent decision in *Boy Scouts of America v. Dale* (2000), it was unclear whether an expressive or religious organization's constitutional rights to freedom of association would "trump" the state's generally applicable anti-discrimination policies. If not, then the consequences for religious groups that exclude "protected" individuals for religious reasons could be disastrous. Sincere scriptural objections to certain behaviors could be swept aside in the interest of "tolerance" and "diversity," and religious student groups could be required to conform to contemporary campus policies or be forced to disband.

Boy Scouts involved a gay former Eagle Scout's attempt to challenge the Boy Scouts' ban on gay scoutmasters. James Dale, the gay scout, argued that the anti-discrimination provisions of New Jersey's public accommodation law compelled the Boy Scouts to alter their policy. "Public accommodation laws" ban discrimination in "public" places. The classic public accommodation laws, for example, ban discrimination on the basis of race and gender in restaurants, hotels, and stores. Historically, public accommodation laws were adopted for the beneficial purpose of making it possible for members of racial minorities, particularly black Americans, to travel from state to state and to be able to purchase services—in hotels, restaurants, and the like—that were available to white citizens. Recently, however, public accommodation laws have been used to ban discrimination even in private clubs. New Jersey's public accommodation law included a ban on discrimination on the basis of sexual orientation. The expansion of public accommodation laws in order to restrict the First Amendment rights of speech and religion is a relatively new phenomenon that has become subject to considerable debate, criticism, and litigation.

The U.S. Supreme Court—in response to New Jersey's use of public accommodation law to force the Boy Scouts to alter its policies—reaffirmed its commitment to freedom of association. It stated that "implicit in the right to engage in activities protected by the First Amendment is a corresponding right to associate with others in pursuit of a wide variety of political, social, economic, educational, *religious,* and cultural ends [emphasis added]." This right, the Court proclaimed, is "crucial in preventing the majority from imposing its views on groups that would rather express other, perhaps unpopular, ideas." Consequently, the Court held that the "forced inclusion of an unwanted person [in this particular case, an openly gay scout] infringes the group's freedom of expressive association if the presence of that person affects in a significant way the group's ability to advocate public or private viewpoints."

As a consequence of the *Boy Scouts* decision, a public university simply may not use its anti-discrimination policies to dictate the leadership or membership of religious organizations. If a public university allows expressive organizations to exist at all, then it must allow religious organizations to exist, to select their own leaders, and to order their own affairs. Furthermore, if a private university claims that federal or state law *compels* it to coerce religious organizations on the basis of such anti-discrimination policies, it is demonstrably wrong. In the words of the U.S. Supreme Court, "While the law is free to promote all sorts of conduct in place of harmful behavior, it is not free to interfere with speech for no better reason than promoting an approved message or discouraging a disfavored one, however enlightened either purpose may strike the government."

Summary of Religious Rights on Public Campuses

If a public university permits expressive organizations to exist at all, then the following basic rights belong to religious organizations as well:

1) Equal access (with other expressive organizations) to campus facilities;
2) equal access to university funding;
3) freedom from university interference in the campus religious group's internal governance and composition; and
4) basic due process of law before any rights or privileges are revoked, even for legitimate reasons. ("Due process of law" is a constitutional requirement that governments must provide individuals or organizations with notice and with an opportunity to be heard before they are deprived of "life, liberty, or property.")

Religious Freedom in the Private University

The administrators of private universities often behave as if their freedom from constitutional restrictions gives them complete discretion and free rein to destroy student liberty. They enact speech codes, they apply rules unequally, and they seemingly punish and discriminate against religious individuals and groups at will. However, as increasing numbers of students have fought back against university abuse of authority and outright oppression—often with the help of FIRE— private universities are beginning to understand the civic and legal realities. While private universities are not bound by constitutional constraints, state laws often substantially restrict their ability to engage in "Star Chamber" practices. (Courts of Star Chamber—secretive, violating accepted rules of fairness, and determined to protect the goals of power—were used in Tudor England against the perceived enemies of the Crown). Public opinion and the courts are becoming less and less inclined to put up with bigoted disciplinary actions aimed against those who dissent from campus orthodoxy, with double standards, and with the duplicity and outright fraud that have come to characterize private university judicial procedures and administrative repression.

As noted, secular liberal arts institutions increasingly behave as if they exist for the purpose of advancing a particular orthodoxy. This political orthodoxy also protects and serves the careers of college administrators, who are loathe to risk the demonstrations and bad academic publicity that they fear would follow their support of equal freedom over the cause of a particular, currently favored political position. By purging and punishing their campuses of all who are not sincere or apparent "true believers," these colleges and universities are much more repressive than a Bob Jones University or other admittedly sectarian school. Unlike those honestly sectarian schools, however, they still advertise themselves to the public as "diverse" institutions dedicated to a "free exchange of ideas." The vulnerability of college administrators at such liberal arts institutions is precisely the gulf between their public self-presentation (academic freedom, free speech, and the protection of individual conscience) and their practice. If a private college admitted in its catalogue that it was devoted to a particular established orthodoxy, and that it would assign rights unequally, it would have considerably more leeway to impose its views on the students who gave their informed consent by attending.

Despite a seeming tidal wave of politically correct orthodoxy on the modern campus, there still is hope for civil liberties, including the indispensable liberty of freedom of religion. Private colleges and universities may not deprive you of your legal rights in a society of law. Indeed, legal doctrines long reserved for more traditional commercial arrangements now have new applicability to the campus setting, and they may be used on behalf of the rights of belief and conscience. Let us handcuff the new and bigoted thought police with not only the requirements of fair process and good faith, but also, indeed, with the ancient and enduring maxims of civilized contract law.

To prevail in the battle for freedom, besieged members of the university community must understand and apply several appropriate legal doctrines. These doctrines, as noted, can vary from state to state, but enough common principles exist to provide some general guidance. For those who treasure liberty, the law can still provide a refuge (although, as we shall discuss later, resort to publicity and the court of public opinion provides additional, powerful assistance, because university administrators are hard pressed to admit and justify publicly the private basis of their actions). The strength of that refuge depends on multiple factors—the laws of the individual state where the university is located; the content of university catalogues, handbooks, and disciplinary rules; and the precise governance and funding of the institution.

Individual State Laws

In our federal system, states have remarkably diverse legal systems. Your rights can vary tremendously from state to state. However, the U.S. Constitution limits the extent to which all states can regulate the private universities in their midst, since the Bill of Rights (which applies to both the states and to the federal government) protects private institutions from excessive government interference. In particular, the First Amendment protects the academic freedom of colleges and universities at least as much as (and frequently more than) it protects the individuals at those institutions.

Decent societies have found ways to protect individuals from indecent behavior. State law often reflects that, and it is particularly relevant to how a university applies its policies and to how university officials behave toward students (and faculty). For example, some states have formulated common-law rules for associations—which include private universities—that prohibit "arbitrary or capricious" decision-making and that require organizations, at an absolute minimum, *to follow their own rules* and to deal in good faith with their members. These standards can be profoundly valuable defenses of liberty in the politically super-charged environment of the modern campus, where discipline without notice or hearing is commonplace.

It is not uncommon for students or groups that deviate from campus orthodoxy to be essentially "railroaded" off campus. Campus officials or judicial courts might hold closed, late-night meetings; they might not inform accused students or groups of the charges against them; they might not offer protection from threats and intimidation to "offensive" students holding poorly understood religious views. It may also be the case that, while several other individuals have committed the same offense, or other groups have the same policies, you and your group are the only ones prosecuted. In such cases, you may be able to force the university literally to take a step back and begin to apply some basically fair procedures. Good faith requires fair process and often prohibits extremes of arbitrary decision-making.

State law also provides common-law rules against *misrepresentation*. Simply put, there is a long tradition of laws against fraud and deceit. Very often, a university's recruiting materials, brochures, and even its "admitted student" orientations—designed to entice you to attend that institution rather than another—will trumpet a school's commitment to "diversity," "inclusion," and "tolerance." Sometimes religious students will be personally assured that they will find a "home" or be "welcome" in the campus community. Promises such as these will often induce religious students to bypass opportunities (and even scholarships) at other schools and to enroll in the private secular university. If those promises of "tolerance" or of a place in the community later turn out to be demonstrably false, a university could find itself in serious legal jeopardy.

There are legal doctrines with strange-sounding names, such as "promissory estoppel," "detrimental reliance," and "fraudulent inducement," that prevent real abuses, such as your being deprived of the promised rights and goods on which you relied in accepting someone's offer. If a university promises you religious liberty and legal equality, and you rely on that promise, causing you to pass up other opportunities, the university may not walk away from its inducement. A university has no right to let you make a decision based on its enticements and then renege on its obligations. To say the least, it may not promise you lawful religious liberty and then put you on trial for exercising it. Private universities may rightfully be beyond the reach of the Constitution, but they have no license to deceive you with false promises. In short, prohibitions against fraudulent inducement to contract and against false advertising can be used to force a change in an administration's behavior. Furthermore, such prohibitions could also be a source of substantial monetary damages for the wronged student, serving as a deterrent that would protect the rights and dignity of others.

When applying to a college or university, ask for its specific policies on religious liberty, nondiscrimination on the basis of religion, and legal equality. If you are already at an institution, and you find yourself or your religious organization subjected to disciplinary action, you immediately should look very closely at university promotional materials, brochures, and Web sites. You also should attempt to recollect (and to confirm with others) any specific conversations you may have had with university officials regarding your religious freedom. If those promises or inducements are clear enough, then a court may very well hold the university to its word. As noted, state common law and statutes vary greatly, but almost every state offers serious protection from outright fraud.

It is very common for religious individuals who dissent from the campus orthodoxy concerning Scripture and sexuality to be the victims of hate campaigns and verbal abuse. Just as religious students should have the right to bear witness to their beliefs, of course, it is the right of the critics of such religious students to express their views and to bear their own moral witness. The crucial issue here is that the same rules should apply equally to all. For example, at Tufts, various student organizations covered the campus with anti-Christian graffiti and hurled terms of abuse at religious minorities. They told demonstrable falsehoods about the TCF. If the members of the TCF had engaged in similar behavior toward gay and lesbian groups, the judicial wrath of the University would have fallen upon them with a vengeance. The TCF might be charged with "homophobia"—for its sincere religious belief that homosexual acts are sinful—but its critics never would be charged with anti-Christian bigotry. Only one group is expected to change its beliefs and the lawful behaviors that follow from those beliefs. Such a double standard violates all promises of legal equality, nondiscrimination on the basis of creed, and religious liberty.

While the law does not protect either minority religions or minority lifestyles from harmful statements of opinion, it does protect individuals from certain kinds of *demonstrably false* assertions and accusations. State laws prohibit libel, slander, and defamation (although too many of us confuse hurtful opinion with these torts). Further, if a campaign against you turns truly vicious, involving, for example, physical intimidation, harassing phone calls, and improper inquiries into confidential information, then you may be the victim of impermissible and punishable acts. You have legal protection from unlawful terroristic threats, intentional infliction of emotional distress, invasion of privacy, or actual harassment. Again, in all of these matters, your rights and protections, in circumstances of promised legal equality, should be the same as those of all others.

University Catalogs, Handbooks, and Disciplinary Rules

Ironically, the very universities that persecute religious minorities may also be their best source of protection. The reason for this is simple and revealing: most private, secular universities make broad and glowing statements about the protected rights of their own students. They have chosen to describe themselves to the world as decent institutions dedicated to fairness, the search for truth, tolerance, and legal equality.

Many of the catalogs, student handbooks, and disciplinary codes of private universities promise nondiscrimination on the basis of religion, freedom of speech and association, and a judicial system with fair hearings prior to any disciplinary action. While it is a source of considerable aggravation for many students to observe the rank hypocrisy of colleges and universities that state and then ignore such self-presentations, these public assurances nonetheless provide ample opportunity for forcing them to follow the principles that they advertise and preach.

As a general rule, *if a university has stated a policy in writing, a court will require the university to adhere to that policy.* Most state courts hold that the contents of university catalogues and handbooks constitute, at least to some degree, contracts between the university and its students. While other state courts have stated that the university and its students are not in a contractual relationship, most of these states—through the use of other legal theories—still require universities to comply with the terms of their own documents. Often, perceiving an inequality in bargaining power between the university (which drew up the contract) and the student, many courts will resolve any ambiguities in the language of the contract in favor of the student.

Unfortunately, the contents of these contracts are rapidly changing, often upon the advice of lawyers paid to reduce a college's exposure to liability from lawsuits (rather than help the colleges live up to their historic obligations to academic freedom and the rights of conscience). Instead of providing blanket free-speech rights to their students, universities now improvise speech codes—usually found in the "verbal conduct" or "verbal behavior" sections of harassment policies. Furthermore, instead of providing students with fair hearings, universities increasingly hold secret proceedings. However, even the most repressive universities can provide their students with a surprising amount of rights, because even the cleverest lawyers have difficulty wiping out from a college catalog all of the high phrases about liberty and fairness with which colleges like to present themselves publicly to the world.

The situation at Tufts presents an excellent example of how handbooks can affect and protect students, even at universities with selective and politically orthodox harassment and antidiscrimination policies. Tufts' student handbook stated that it was university policy not to discriminate on the basis of religion. It also stated that Tufts respected the freedom of association. It also stated, however, that student organizations were not allowed to discriminate on the basis of (among other things) religion and sexual orientation. Tufts was remarkably unaware of the profound conflict among these various principles. Above all, it is simply impossible for a university to respect freedom of association and religious freedom while simultaneously prohibiting religious groups from using religious criteria as a basis for selecting members, let alone leaders.

Although the handbooks were confusing about the true extent of the TCF's religious liberties, it was clear enough the Judiciary's secret, late-night meeting violated the TCF's rights to fair process. The student handbooks provided for at least two sets of open hearings, before impartial tribunals, before any student organization could be punished for violating school rules. It was on this basis—once Tufts was reeling from FIRE's public exposure of the case—that a university appeals panel reversed the Judiciary's decision and re-recognized the TCF. At later hearings, the TCF's ability to cite its rights as set forth in Tufts' handbooks prevented a host of further injustices and proved instrumental in securing the TCF's eventual victory.

If you find yourself or your organization facing university discipline, or if you find that the university is trying to impose new and discriminatory policies on you, it is absolutely *critical* that you read *every word* of the university's handbooks and catalogs. Indeed, don't stop with these documents. Search the school's Web site thoroughly. Pick up copies of its admissions materials. Many courts will be sympathetic to the argument that your tens of thousands of tuition dollars buy you not just an education but also good faith adherence to your school's written policies. Even if administrators don't realize the importance of following the rules, their lawyers almost certainly will. If not, then many judges will.

University Governance and Funding

A final source of possible legal protection for a student at a private university lies in a particularly difficult legal and political area, namely, the extent of the government's involvement in the financing and governance of a school. If that involvement goes beyond a certain point, it is possible that the school will be deemed, for legal purposes, "public," and in that case, all constitutional protections will apply. This happened, for example, at the University of Pittsburgh and at Temple University, both in Pennsylvania. State laws there required that, in return for significant public funding, a certain number of state officials must serve on the school's boards. That fact led these formerly "private" universities to be treated, legally, as "public." In fact, however, this is a very rare occurrence, and the odds of any private school that you attend being deemed legally public are very slim. Unless your school is officially public, you always should assume that the Constitution will not apply there.

There are many students, faculty members, and even lawyers who believe, wholly erroneously, that if a college receives *any* federal or state funding, it is therefore "public." In fact, accepting governmental funds usually makes the university subject *only* to the conditions—sometimes broad, sometimes narrow—specifically attached to the use of those specific funds. (The two most prominent conditions attached to all federal funding are nondiscrimination on the basis of race and nondiscrimination on the basis of gender.) Furthermore, the "strings" attached to virtually all grants of federal funds are not always helpful to the cause of liberty, which is one reason that people who worry about excessive government power can be opposed to governmental funding of private colleges and universities.

In terms of the law, there are two facts to keep in mind here. First, no federal funding of a private college or institution requires that the recipient honor the First Amendment. Second, receiving a large percentage of total funds from the government does not convert a school from private to public. Indeed, the Supreme Court has held that even 99 percent government funding does not, by itself, make a school public.

That should not stop you, however, from learning as much as you can about the funding and governance of your institution. Do the taxpayers truly want to subsidize assaults upon religious liberty? Do members of the Board of Trustees truly want to be party to such assaults? Do donors want to pay for an attack on a liberty that most Americans hold so dear? Information about funding and governance is vital and useful. For example, you may find that a major foundation is a substantial source of contributed funds to your college, and you may undertake to contact that foundation to report on how the university selectively abuses the rights and consciences of students of faith. Colleges are *extremely* sensitive to contributors learning about official bigotry and injustice at the institutions they support.

Summary of Religious Rights on Private Campuses

Because private colleges have such broad freedom to determine their own policies—and because state laws vary so widely—it is best to speak only of having "potential" rights on a private campus. However, the following generalizations can be made with a certain confidence. Unless you have given informed consent to be part of a voluntary association in which you have waived these rights:

1) You have the right to rational, nonarbitrary disciplinary proceedings and, to a lesser extent, to rational, nonarbitrary results;
2) You have the right to receive treatment equal to those who have engaged in similar behavior;
3) You have the right to honesty and good faith from university officials; and
4) You have the right to enjoy all of the rights promised you by university catalogs, handbooks, and disciplinary codes.

ABOUT THE AUTHOR

David French is a graduate of Harvard Law School and has extensive experience representing Christian individuals, ministries, churches, and schools. David has taught at Cornell Law School. He is the author of the Foundation for Individual Rights in Education's *Guide to Religious Liberty on Campus* and is currently in private practice in Lexington, Kentucky.